Jesus and His First Followers

Jesus
and His First Followers

The True Story

by

Luke

A first-century doctor and an eyewitness of some of these events

Copyright 1989
by Baker Book House Company

Part 1 (the Gospel of Luke) and part 2 (the Acts of the Apostles) are from *The Living Bible*, © 1971 owned by assignment by Illinois Regional Bank N.A. (as trustee), and are used by permission of Tyndale House Publishers, Inc., Wheaton, IL 60187.

ISBN: 0-8010-5654-3

Printed in the United States of America

Contents

Introduction

My name is Luke. Often I am called Dr. Luke, for I am a physician by profession. Born of Gentile parents in the Syrian city of Antioch, I received my basic education in literature, history, and medicine. I became a Christian in Antioch when two Jewish teachers, Barnabas and Paul, told me about Jesus of Nazareth. This Jesus, they said, had died on a cross in Jerusalem but had risen from the grave; he appeared to numerous people, and then ascended to heaven, promising that some day he would return.

The story made a deep impression on many people in Antioch, including me. I dedicated my life to Jesus, who is also called Christ. Accompanying Paul on his missionary journeys, I learned many details about the life and teaching of Jesus. And when Paul, after his third missionary tour, was arrested in Jerusalem and imprisoned for two years in Caesarea, I stayed in Israel to gather material for writing a gospel account.

In Jerusalem and the regions of Judea and Galilee, I went to eyewitnesses who were able to give me firsthand reports of the words and deeds of Jesus. For example, I visited Mary the aged mother of Jesus, who told me that she had treasured in her heart everything concerning Jesus' birth and childhood. She related to me his conception and birth and his journey to the temple as a twelve-year-old boy.

Others told me about Jesus' ministry: the sermon he preached in his hometown synagogue of Nazareth; the miraculous catch of fish with Peter's nets and boat; the healing of the centurion's son; the teaching of the numerous parables; the journey to Jerusalem; the calling of Zaccheus and visit to his house; Jesus' arrest, trial, and crucifixion; and, to mention no more, the reports concerning his resurrection from the dead and his ascension into heaven.

I was interested in the life and ministry of Jesus that ended in Jerusalem. But I knew that what Jesus had begun could not be confined to Jerusalem. He came back to life and told his followers to preach repentance and forgiveness of sins not only to Jews in Jerusalem but to people everywhere, in all the nations of the world. In short, he said that this message had universal significance. Thus, in my presentation I tried to stress that truth.

Just before his ascension, Jesus told his immediate followers (who are known as apostles) that they had to wait for the Holy Spirit to descend on them. Then filled with the Spirit, they would have to proclaim Jesus' gospel first in Jerusalem, next in Judea and Samaria, and then everywhere in the world. They would have to go to the *ends of the world,* as Jesus said. He meant Rome, because from this imperial city as the hub of the Roman empire excellent roads extended to every area of the known world.

In the second part of my book, I wrote about the continuation of Jesus' work. On the day of Pentecost (a Jewish holiday), the Holy Spirit descended on the apostles in Jerusalem. Then in ever-widening circles, like ripples created by a stone thrown into a pond, the church began to develop. The gospel came to the Jews first, but later, in God's providence, also to the Samaritans when they received the Holy Spirit. The Samaritans entered the church as members on an equal footing with the Jewish Christians. A few years later, Gentiles in Caesarea received the gift of the Holy Spirit. They also entered the ever-expanding church. So the gospel came to Antioch, where I first heard it from the lips of Barnabas and Paul.

These two teachers left Antioch and went first to Cyprus and then to Asia Minor. They preached the gospel in the cities of Pisidian Antioch, Iconium, Lystra, and Derbe. Wherever they went, they founded churches. Multitudes of people, mostly Gentiles, heard the good news of salvation. Consequently the church outside Israel became a Gentile church. The apostles kept the unity of the church when they ruled that Gentile Christians, of whom I am one, did not have to submit to Jewish rules and regulations. They said that faith in Jesus was sufficient for salvation.

Bolstered by that rule, Paul took the gospel from the continent of Asia to the continent of Europe. When he came to Macedonia, I was with him. He went to the population centers of Philippi, Thessalonica, Athens, and Corinth. In those cities he preached the gospel, with the result that the church began to develop throughout Europe. Paul wanted to go to Spain and on his way visit the Christian church in Rome. However, his plans were delayed because of an extended imprisonment in Caesarea. His stay there ended when he appealed to the emperor. As a prisoner, he was sent to Rome to stand trial. In Rome he was acquitted and released after a two-year period of house arrest.

While composing my book, I have tried to be evenhanded. For example, in part 1 I give equal attention to men and women: Zacharias and Elizabeth, Joseph and Mary, Simeon and Anna, Jairus and his daughter, the widow of Nain and her son, the shepherd who lost a sheep and the woman who lost a coin, the man who planted a mustard seed and the woman who made bread. In part 2 I have tried to present the labors of both Peter and Paul. In fact, these two apostles have had some parallel experiences: both healed a cripple, one in Jerusalem and one in Lystra; both raised a dead person, one in Joppa and one in Troas; and both escaped from prison, Peter in Jerusalem and Paul in Philippi.

In writing my book I have experienced God's guiding care and oversight. To illustrate: part 1 begins with Jesus' birth and ends with his ascension. This is a period of 33 years. Part 2 begins with Jesus' ascension and concludes with Paul's release from Roman imprisonment. This, too, is a period of 33 years.

Therefore, guided by God's Holy Spirit in my research and writing, I have presented in part 1 an accurate account of what Jesus said and did during his earthly ministry. And I have continued this account in part 2, showing how through the preaching of the good news, the church began to develop first in Jerusalem and afterward in Samaria, Syria, Asia Minor, and Europe. In fact the conclusion to my book is an open-ended one, saying that the preaching of God's kingdom and the teaching about Jesus Christ continue without hindrance.

Dr. Simon J. Kistemaker
Jackson, Mississippi

Part 1

The True Story of Jesus

1

Dear friend who loves God:

Several biographies of Christ have already been written using as their source material the reports circulating among us from the early disciples and other eyewitnesses. However, it occurred to me that it would be well to recheck all these accounts from first to last and after thorough investigation to pass this summary on to you, to reassure you of the truth of all you were taught.

My story begins with a Jewish priest, Zacharias, who lived when Herod was king of Judea. Zacharias was a member of the Abijah division of the Temple service corps. (His wife Elizabeth was, like himself, a member of the priest tribe of the Jews, a descendant of Aaron.) Zacharias and Elizabeth were godly folk, careful to obey all of God's laws in spirit as well as in letter. But they had no children, for Elizabeth was barren; and now they were both very old.

One day as Zacharias was going about his work in the Temple—for his division was on duty that week—the honor fell to him by lot to enter the inner sanctuary and burn incense before the Lord. Meanwhile, a great crowd stood outside in the Temple court, praying as they always did during that part of the service when the incense was being burned.

Zacharias was in the sanctuary when suddenly an angel appeared, standing to the right of the altar of incense! Zacharias was startled and terrified.

But the angel said, "Don't be afraid, Zacharias! For I have come to tell you that God has heard your prayer, and your wife Elizabeth will bear you a son! And you are to name him John. You will both have great joy and gladness at his birth, and many will rejoice with you. For he will be one of the Lord's great men. He must never touch wine or hard liquor—and he will be filled with the Holy Spirit, even from before his birth! And he will persuade many a Jew to turn to the Lord his God. He will be a man of rugged spirit and power like Elijah, the prophet of old; and he will precede the coming of the Messiah, preparing the people for his arrival. He will soften adult hearts to become like little children's, and will change disobedient minds to the wisdom of faith."

Zacharias said to the angel, "But this is impossible! I'm an old man now, and my wife is also well along in years."

Then the angel said, "I am Gabriel! I stand in the very presence of God. It was he who sent me to you with this good news! And now, because you haven't believed me, you are to be stricken silent, unable to speak until the child is born. For my words will certainly come true at the proper time."

Meanwhile the crowds outside were waiting for Zacharias to appear and wondered why he was taking so long. When he finally came out, he couldn't speak to them, and they realized from his gestures that he must have seen a vision in the Temple. He stayed on at the Temple for the remaining days of his Temple duties and then returned home. Soon afterwards Elizabeth his wife became pregnant and went into seclusion for five months.

"How kind the Lord is," she exclaimed, "to take away my disgrace of having no children!"

The following month God sent the angel Gabriel to Nazareth, a village in Galilee, to a virgin, Mary, engaged to be married to a man named Joseph, a descendant of King David.

Gabriel appeared to her and said, "Congratulations, favored lady! The Lord is with you!"

Confused and disturbed, Mary tried to think what the angel could mean.

"Don't be frightened, Mary," the angel told her, "for God has decided to wonderfully bless you! Very soon now, you will become pregnant and have a baby boy, and you are to name him 'Jesus.' He shall be very great and shall be called the Son of God. And the Lord God shall give him the throne of his ancestor David. And he shall reign over Israel forever; his Kingdom shall never end!"

Mary asked the angel, "But how can I have a baby? I am a virgin."

The angel replied, "The Holy Spirit shall come upon you, and the power of God shall overshadow you; so the baby born to you will be utterly holy—the Son of God. Furthermore, six months ago your Aunt Elizabeth—'the barren one,' they called her—became pregnant in her old age! For every promise from God shall surely come true."

Mary said, "I am the Lord's servant, and I am willing to do whatever he wants. May everything you said come true." And then the angel disappeared.

A few days later Mary hurried to the highlands of Judea to the town where Zacharias lived, to visit Elizabeth.

At the sound of Mary's greeting, Elizabeth's child leaped within her and she was filled with the Holy Spirit.

She gave a glad cry and exclaimed to Mary, "You are favored by God above all other women, and your child is destined for God's mightiest praise. What an honor this is, that the mother of my Lord should visit me! When you came in and greeted me, the instant I heard your voice, my baby moved in me for joy! You believed that God would do what he said; that is why he has given you this wonderful blessing."

Mary responded, "Oh, how I praise the Lord. How I rejoice in God my Savior! For he took notice of his lowly servant girl, and now generation after generation forever shall call me blest of God. For he, the mighty Holy One, has done great things to me. His mercy goes on from generation to generation, to all who reverence him.

"How powerful is his mighty arm! How he scatters the proud and haughty ones! He has torn princes from their thrones and exalted the lowly. He has satisfied the hungry hearts and sent the rich away with empty hands. And how he has helped his servant Israel! He has not forgotten his promise to be merciful. For he promised our fathers—Abraham and his children—to be merciful to them forever."

Mary stayed with Elizabeth about three months and then went back to her own home.

By now Elizabeth's waiting was over, for the time had come for the baby to be born—and it was a boy. The word spread quickly to her neighbors and relatives of how kind the Lord had been to her, and everyone rejoiced.

When the baby was eight days old, all the relatives and friends came for the circumcision ceremony. They all assumed the baby's name would be Zacharias, after his father.

But Elizabeth said, "No! He must be named John!"

"What?" they exclaimed. "There is no one in all your family by that name." So they asked the baby's father, talking to him by gestures.

He motioned for a piece of paper and to everyone's surprise wrote, "His name is *John!*" Instantly Zacharias could speak again, and he began praising God.

Wonder fell upon the whole neighborhood, and the news of what had happened spread through the Judean hills. And everyone who heard about it thought long thoughts and asked, "I wonder what this child will turn out to be? For the hand of the Lord is surely upon him in some special way."

Then his father Zacharias was filled with the Holy Spirit and gave this prophecy:

"Praise the Lord, the God of Israel, for he has come to visit his people and has redeemed them. He is sending us a Mighty Savior from the royal line of his servant David, just as he promised through his holy prophets long ago—someone to save us from our enemies, from all who hate us.

"He has been merciful to our ancestors, yes, to Abraham himself, by remembering his sacred promise to him, and by granting us the privilege of serving God fearlessly, freed from our enemies, and by making us holy and acceptable, ready to stand in his presence forever.

"And you, my little son, shall be called the prophet of the glorious God, for you will prepare the way for the Messiah. You will tell his people how to find salvation through forgiveness of their sins. All this will be because the mercy of our God is very tender, and heaven's dawn is about to break upon us, to give light to those who sit in darkness and death's shadow, and to guide us to the path of peace."

The little boy greatly loved God and when he grew up he lived out in the lonely wilderness until he began his public ministry to Israel.

2

About this time Caesar Augustus, the Roman Emperor, decreed that a census should be taken throughout the nation. (This census was taken when Quirinius was governor of Syria.)

Everyone was required to return to his ancestral home for this registration. And because Joseph was a member of the royal line, he had to go to Bethlehem in Judea, King David's ancient home—journeying there from the Galilean village of Nazareth. He took with him Mary, his fiancée, who was obviously pregnant by this time.

And while they were there, the time came for her baby to be born; and she gave birth to her first child, a son. She wrapped him in a blanket and laid him in a manger, because there was no room for them in the village inn.

That night some shepherds were in the fields outside the village, guarding their flocks of sheep. Suddenly an angel appeared among them, and the landscape shone bright with the glory of the Lord. They were badly frightened, but the angel reassured them.

"Don't be afraid!" he said. "I bring you the most joyful news ever announced, and it is for everyone! The Savior—yes, the Messiah, the Lord—has been born tonight in Bethlehem! How will you recognize him? You will find a baby wrapped in a blanket, lying in a manger!"

Suddenly, the angel was joined by a vast host of others—the armies of heaven—praising God:

"Glory to God in the highest heaven," they sang, "and peace on earth for all those pleasing him."

When this great army of angels had returned again to heaven, the shepherds said to each other, "Come on! Let's go to Bethlehem! Let's see this wonderful thing that has happened, which the Lord has told us about."

They ran to the village and found their way to Mary and Joseph. And there was the baby, lying in the manger. The shepherds told everyone what had happened and what the angel had said to them about this child. All who heard the shepherds' story expressed astonishment, but Mary quietly treasured these things in her heart and often thought about them.

Then the shepherds went back again to their fields and flocks, praising God for the visit of the angels, and because they had seen the child, just as the angel had told them.

Eight days later, at the baby's circumcision ceremony, he was named Jesus, the name given him by the angel before he was even conceived.

When the time came for Mary's purification offering at the Temple, as required by the laws of Moses after the birth of a child, his parents took him to Jerusalem to present him to the Lord; for in these laws God had said, "If a woman's first child is a boy, he shall be dedicated to the Lord."

At that time Jesus' parents also offered their sacrifice for purification—"either a pair of turtledoves or two young pigeons" was the legal requirement. That day a man named Simeon, a Jerusalem resident, was in the Temple. He was a good man, very devout, filled with the Holy Spirit and constantly expecting the Messiah to come soon. For the Holy Spirit had revealed to him that he would not die until he had seen him—God's anointed King. The Holy Spirit had impelled him to go to the Temple that day; and so, when Mary and Joseph arrived to present the baby Jesus to the Lord in obedience to the law, Simeon was there and took the child in his arms, praising God.

"Lord," he said, "now I can die content! For I have seen him as you promised me I would. I have seen the Savior you have given to the world. He is the Light that will shine upon the nations, and he will be the glory of your people Israel!"

Joseph and Mary just stood there, marveling at what was being said about Jesus.

Simeon blessed them but then said to Mary, "A sword shall pierce your soul, for this child shall be rejected by many in Israel, and this to their undoing. But he will be the greatest joy of many others. And the deepest thoughts of many hearts shall be revealed."

Anna, a prophetess, was also there in the Temple that day. She was the daughter of Phanuel, of the Jewish tribe of Asher, and was very old, for she had been a widow for eighty-four years following seven years of marriage. She never left the Temple but stayed there night and day, worshiping God by praying and often fasting.

She came along just as Simeon was talking with Mary and Joseph, and she also began thanking God and telling everyone in Jerusalem who had been awaiting the coming of the Savior that the Messiah had finally arrived.

When Jesus' parents had fulfilled all the requirements of the Law of God they returned home to Nazareth in Galilee. There the child became a strong, robust lad, and was known for wisdom beyond his years; and God poured out his blessings on him.

When Jesus was twelve years old he accompanied his parents to Jerusalem for the annual Passover Festival, which they attended each year. After the celebration was over they started home to Nazareth, but Jesus stayed behind in Jerusalem. His parents didn't miss him the first day, for they assumed he was with friends among the other travelers. But when he didn't show up that evening, they started to look for him among their relatives and friends; and when they couldn't find him, they went back to Jerusalem to search for him there.

Three days later they finally discovered him. He was in the Temple, sitting among the teachers of Law, discussing deep questions with them and amazing everyone with his understanding and answers.

His parents didn't know what to think. "Son!" his mother said to him. "Why have you done this to us? Your father and I have been frantic, searching for you everywhere."

"But why did you need to search?" he asked. "Didn't you realize that I would be here at the Temple, in my Father's House?" But they didn't understand what he meant.

Then he returned to Nazareth with them and was obedient to them; and his mother stored away all these things in her heart. So Jesus grew both tall and wise, and was loved by God and man.

3

In the fifteenth year of the reign of Emperor Tiberius Caesar, a message came from God to John (the son of Zacharias), as he was living out in the deserts. (Pilate was governor over Judea at that time; Herod, over Galilee; his brother Philip, over Iturea and Trachonitis; Lysanias, over Abilene; and Annas and Caiaphas were High Priests.) Then John went from place to place on both sides of the Jordan River, preaching that people should be baptized to show that they had turned to God and away from their sins, in order to be forgiven.

In the words of Isaiah the prophet, John was "a voice shouting from the barren wilderness, 'Prepare a road for the Lord to travel on! Widen the pathway before him! Level the mountains! Fill up the valleys! Straighten the curves! Smooth out the ruts! And then all mankind shall see the Savior sent from God.' "

Here is a sample of John's preaching to the crowds that came for baptism: "You brood of snakes! You are trying to escape hell without truly turning to God! That is why you want to be baptized! First go and prove by the way you live that you really have repented. And don't think you are safe because you are descendants of Abraham. That isn't enough. God can produce children of Abraham from these desert stones! The axe of his judgment is poised over you, ready to sever your roots and cut you down. Yes, every tree that does not produce good fruit will be chopped down and thrown into the fire."

The crowd replied, "What do you want us to do?"

"If you have two coats," he replied, "give one to the poor. If you have extra food, give it away to those who are hungry."

Even tax collectors—notorious for their corruption—came to be baptized and asked, "How shall we prove to you that we have abandoned our sins?"

"By your honesty," he replied. "Make sure you collect no more taxes than the Roman government requires you to."

"And us," asked some soldiers, "what about us?"

John replied, "Don't extort money by threats and violence; don't accuse anyone of what you know he didn't do; and be content with your pay!"

Everyone was expecting the Messiah to come soon, and eager to know whether or not John was he. This was the question of the hour, and was being discussed everywhere.

John answered the question by saying, "I baptize only with water; but someone is coming soon who has far higher authority than mine; in fact, I am not even worthy of being his slave. He will baptize you with fire—with the Holy Spirit. He will separate chaff from grain, and burn up the chaff with eternal fire and store away the grain." He used many such warnings as he announced the Good News to the people.

(But after John had publicly criticized Herod, governor of Galilee, for marrying Herodias, his brother's wife, and for many other wrongs he had done, Herod put John in prison, thus adding this sin to all his many others.)

Then one day, after the crowds had been baptized, Jesus himself was baptized; and as he was praying, the heavens opened, and the Holy Spirit in the form of a dove settled upon him, and a voice from heaven said, "You are my much loved Son, yes, my delight."

Jesus was about thirty years old when he began his public ministry.

Jesus was known as the son of Joseph.

Joseph's father was Heli;

Heli's father was Matthat;

Matthat's father was Levi;
Levi's father was Melchi;
Melchi's father was Jannai;
Jannai's father was Joseph;
Joseph's father was Mattathias;
Mattathias' father was Amos;
Amos' father was Nahum;
Nahum's father was Esli;
Esli's father was Naggai;
Naggai's father was Maath;
Maath's father was Mattathias;
Mattathias' father was Semein;
Semein's father was Josech;
Josech's father was Joda;
Joda's father was Joanan;
Joanan's father was Rhesa;
Rhesa's father was Zerubbabel;
Zerubbabel's father was Shealtiel;
Shealtiel's father was Neri;
Neri's father was Melchi;
Melchi's father was Addi;
Addi's father was Cosam;
Cosam's father was Elmadam;
Elmadam's father was Er;
Er's father was Joshua;
Joshua's father was Eliezer;
Eliezer's father was Jorim;
Jorim's father was Matthat;
Matthat's father was Levi;
Levi's father was Simeon;
Simeon's father was Judah;
Judah's father was Joseph;
Joseph's father was Jonam;
Jonam's father was Eliakim;
Eliakim's father was Melea;
Melea's father was Menna;
Menna's father was Mattatha;

Mattatha's father was Nathan;
Nathan's father was David;
David's father was Jesse;
Jesse's father was Obed;
Obed's father was Boaz;
Boaz' father was Salmon;
Salmon's father was Nahshon;
Nahshon's father was Amminadab;
Amminadab's father was Admin;
Admin's father was Arni;
Arni's father was Hezron;
Hezron's father was Perez;
Perez' father was Judah;
Judah's father was Jacob;
Jacob's father was Isaac;
Isaac's father was Abraham;
Abraham's father was Terah;
Terah's father was Nahor;
Nahor's father was Serug;
Serug's father was Reu;
Reu's father was Peleg;
Peleg's father was Eber;
Eber's father was Shelah;
Shelah's father was Cainan;
Cainan's father was Arphaxad;
Arphaxad's father was Shem;
Shem's father was Noah;
Noah's father was Lamech;
Lamech's father was Methuselah;
Methuselah's father was Enoch;
Enoch's father was Jared;
Jared's father was Mahalaleel;
Mahalaleel's father was Cainan;
Cainan's father was Enos;
Enos' father was Seth;
Seth's father was Adam;
Adam's father was God.

4

Then Jesus, full of the Holy Spirit, left the Jordan River, being urged by the Spirit out into the barren wastelands of Judea, where Satan tempted him for forty days. He ate nothing all that time, and was very hungry.

Satan said, "If you are God's Son, tell this stone to become a loaf of bread."

But Jesus replied, "It is written in the Scriptures, 'Other things in life are much more important than bread!' "

Then Satan took him up and revealed to him all the kingdoms of the world in a moment of time; and the devil told him, "I will give you all these splendid kingdoms and their glory—for they are mine to give to anyone I wish—if you will only get down on your knees and worship me."

Jesus replied, "We must worship God, and him alone. So it is written in the Scriptures."

Then Satan took him to Jerusalem to a high roof of the Temple and said, "If you are the Son of God, jump off! For the Scriptures say that God will send his angels to guard you and to keep you from crashing to the pavement below!"

Jesus replied, "The Scriptures also say, 'Do not put the Lord your God to a foolish test.' "

When the devil had ended all the temptations, he left Jesus for a while and went away.

Then Jesus returned to Galilee, full of the Holy Spirit's power. Soon he became well known throughout all that region for his sermons in the synagogues; everyone praised him.

When he came to the village of Nazareth, his boyhood home, he went as usual to the synagogue on Saturday, and stood up to read the Scriptures. The book of Isaiah the prophet was handed to him, and he opened it to the place where it says:

"The Spirit of the Lord is upon me; he has appointed me to preach Good News to the poor; he has sent me to heal the brokenhearted and to announce that captives shall be released and the blind shall see, that the downtrodden shall be freed from their oppressors, and that God is ready to give blessings to all who come to him."

He closed the book and handed it back to the attendant and sat down, while everyone in the synagogue gazed at him intently. Then he added, "These Scriptures came true today!"

All who were there spoke well of him and were amazed by the beautiful words that fell from his lips. "How can this be?" they asked. "Isn't this Joseph's son?"

Then he said, "Probably you will quote me that proverb, 'Physician, heal yourself'—meaning, 'Why don't you do miracles here in your home town like those you did in Capernaum?' But I solemnly declare to you that no prophet is accepted in his own home town! For example, remember how Elijah the prophet used a miracle to help the widow of Zarephath—a foreigner from the land of Sidon. There were many Jewish widows needing help in those days of famine, for there had been no rain for three and one-half years, and hunger stalked the land; yet Elijah was not sent to them. Or think of the prophet Elisha, who healed Naaman, a Syrian, rather than the many Jewish lepers needing help."

These remarks stung them to fury; and jumping up, they mobbed him and took him to the edge of the hill on which the city was built, to push him over the cliff. But he walked away through the crowd and left them.

Then he returned to Capernaum, a city in Galilee, and preached there in the synagogue every Saturday. Here, too, the people were amazed at the things he said. For he spoke as one who knew the truth, instead of merely quoting the opinions of others as his authority.

Once as he was teaching in the synagogue, a man possessed by a demon began shouting at Jesus, "Go away! We want nothing to do with you, Jesus from Nazareth. You have come to destroy us. I know who you are—the Holy Son of God."

Jesus cut him short. "Be silent!" he told the demon. "Come out!" The demon threw the man to the floor as the crowd watched, and then left him without hurting him futher.

Amazed, the people asked, "What is in this man's words that even demons obey him?" The story of what he had done spread like wildfire throughout the whole region.

After leaving the synagogue that day, he went to Simon's home where he found Simon's mother-in-law very sick with a high fever. "Please heal her," everyone begged.

Standing at her bedside he spoke to the fever, rebuking it, and immediately her temperature returned to normal and she got up and prepared a meal for them!

As the sun went down that evening, all the villagers who had any sick people in their homes, no matter what their diseases were, brought them to Jesus; and the touch of his hands healed every one! Some were possessed by demons; and the demons came out at his command, shouting, "You are the Son of God." But because they knew he was the Christ, he stopped them and told them to be silent.

Early the next morning he went out into the desert. The crowds searched everywhere for him and when they finally found him they begged him not to leave them, but to stay at Capernaum. But he replied, "I must preach the Good News of the Kingdom of God in other places too, for that is why I was sent." So he continued to travel around preaching in the synagogues throughout Judea.

5

One day as he was preaching on the shore of Lake Gennesaret, great crowds pressed in on him to listen to the Word of God. He noticed two empty boats standing at the water's edge while the fishermen washed their nets. Stepping into one of the boats, Jesus asked Simon, its owner, to push out a little into the water, so that he could sit in the boat and speak to the crowds from there.

When he had finished speaking, he said to Simon, "Now go out where it is deeper and let down your nets and you will catch a lot of fish!"

"Sir," Simon replied, "we worked hard all last night and didn't catch a thing. But if you say so, we'll try again."

And this time their nets were so full that they began to tear! A shout for help brought their partners in the other boat and soon both boats were filled with fish and on the verge of sinking.

When Simon Peter realized what had happened, he fell to his knees before Jesus and said, "Oh, sir, please leave us—I'm too much of a sinner for you to have around." For he was awestruck by the size of their catch, as were the others with him, and his partners too—James and John, the sons of Zebedee. Jesus replied, "Don't be afraid! From now on you'll be fishing for the souls of men!"

And as soon as they landed, they left everything and went with him.

One day in a certain village he was visiting, there was a man with an advanced case of leprosy. When he saw Jesus he fell to the ground before him, face downward in the dust, begging to be healed.

"Sir," he said, "if you only will, you can clear me of every trace of my disease."

Jesus reached out and touched the man and said, "Of course I will. Be healed." And the leprosy left him instantly! Then Jesus instructed him to go at once without telling anyone what had happened and be examined by the Jewish priest. "Offer the sacrifice Moses' law requires for lepers who are healed," he said. "This will prove to everyone that you are well." Now the report of his power spread even faster and vast crowds came to hear him preach and to be healed of their diseases. But he often withdrew to the wilderness for prayer.

One day while he was teaching, some Jewish religious leaders and teachers of the Law were sitting nearby. (It seemed that these men showed up from every village in all Galilee and Judea, as well as from Jerusalem.) And the Lord's healing power was upon him.

Then—look! Some men came carrying a paralyzed man on a sleeping mat. They tried to push through the crowd to Jesus but couldn't reach him. So they went up on the roof above him, took off some tiles and lowered the sick man down into the crowd, still on his sleeping mat, right in front of Jesus.

Seeing their faith, Jesus said to the man, "My friend, your sins are forgiven!"

"Who does this fellow think he is?" the Pharisees and teachers of the Law exclaimed among themselves. "This is blasphemy! Who but God can forgive sins?"

Jesus knew what they were thinking, and he replied, "Why is it blasphemy? I, the Messiah, have the authority on earth to forgive sins. But talk is cheap—anybody could say that. So I'll prove it to you by healing this man." Then, turning to the paralyzed man, he commanded, "Pick up your stretcher and go on home, for you are healed!"

And immediately, as everyone watched, the man jumped to his feet, picked up his mat and went home praising God! Everyone present was gripped with awe and fear. And they praised God, remarking over and over again, "We have seen strange things today."

Later on as Jesus left the town he saw a tax collector—with the usual reputation for cheating—sitting at a tax collection booth. The man's name was Levi. Jesus said to him, "Come and be one of my disciples!" So Levi left everything, sprang up and went with him.

Soon Levi held a reception in his home with Jesus as the guest of honor. Many of Levi's fellow tax collectors and other guests were there.

But the Pharisees and teachers of the Law complained bitterly to Jesus' disciples about his eating with such notorious sinners.

Jesus answered them, "It is the sick who need a doctor, not those in good health. My purpose is to invite sinners to turn from their sins, not to spend my time with those who think themselves already good enough."

Their next complaint was that Jesus' disciples were feasting instead of fasting. "John the Baptist's disciples are constantly going without food, and praying," they declared, "and so do the disciples of the Pharisees. Why are yours wining and dining?"

Jesus asked, "Do happy men fast? Do wedding guests go hungry while celebrating with the groom? But the time will come when the bridegroom will be killed; then they won't want to eat."

Then Jesus used this illustration: "No one tears off a piece of a new garment to make a patch for an old one. Not only will the new garment be ruined, but the old garment will look worse with a new patch on it! And no one puts new wine into old wineskins, for the new wine bursts the old skins, ruining the skins and spilling the wine. New wine must be put into new wineskins. But no one after drinking the old wine seems to want the fresh and the new. 'The old ways are best,' they say."

6

One Sabbath as Jesus and his disciples were walking through some grainfields, they were breaking off the heads of wheat, rubbing off the husks in their hands and eating the grains.

But some Pharisees said, "That's illegal! Your disciples are harvesting grain, and it's against the Jewish law to work on the Sabbath."

Jesus replied, "Don't you read the Scriptures? Haven't you ever read what King David did when he and his men were hungry? He went into the Temple and took the shewbread, the special bread that was placed before the Lord, and ate it—illegal as this was—and shared it with others." And Jesus added, "I am master even of the Sabbath."

On another Sabbath he was in the synagogue teaching, and a man was present whose right hand was deformed. The teachers of the Law and the Pharisees watched closely to see whether he would heal the man that day, since it was the Sabbath. For they were eager to find some charge to bring against him.

How well he knew their thoughts! But he said to the man with the deformed hand, "Come and stand here where everyone can see." So he did.

Then Jesus said to the Pharisees and teachers of the Law, "I have a question for you. Is it right to do good on the Sabbath day, or to do harm? To save life, or to destroy it?"

He looked around at them one by one and then said to the man, "Reach out your hand." And as he did, it became completely normal again. At this, the enemies of Jesus were wild with rage, and began to plot his murder.

One day soon afterwards he went out into the mountains to pray, and prayed all night. At daybreak he called together his followers and chose twelve of them to be the inner circle of his disciples. (They were appointed as his "apostles," or "missionaries.") Here are their names:

Simon (he also called him Peter),
Andrew (Simon's brother),
James,
John,
Philip,
Bartholomew,
Matthew,
Thomas,
James (the son of Alphaeus),
Simon (a member of the Zealots, a subversive political party),
Judas (son of James),
Judas Iscariot (who later betrayed him).

When they came down the slopes of the mountain, they stood with Jesus on a large, level area, surrounded by many of his followers who, in turn, were surrounded by the crowds. For people from all over Judea and from Jerusalem and from as far north as the seacoasts of Tyre and Sidon had come to hear him or to be healed. And he cast out many demons. Everyone was trying to touch him, for when they did healing power went out from him and they were cured.

Then he turned to his disciples and said, "What happiness there is for you who are poor, for the Kingdom of God is yours! What happiness there is for you who are now hungry, for you are going to be satisfied! What happiness there is for you who weep, for the time will come when you shall laugh with joy! What happiness it is when others hate you and exclude you and insult you and smear your name because you are mine! When that happens, rejoice! Yes, leap for joy! For you will have a great reward awaiting you in heaven. And you will be in good company—the ancient prophets were treated that way too!

"But, oh, the sorrows that await the rich. For they have their only happiness down here. They are fat and prosperous now, but a time of awful hunger is before them. Their careless laughter now means sorrow then. And what sadness is ahead for those praised by the crowds—for *false* prophets have *always* been praised.

"Listen, all of you. Love your *enemies*. Do *good* to those who *hate* you. Pray for the happiness of those who *curse* you; implore God's blessing on those who *hurt* you.

"If someone slaps you on one cheek, let him slap the other too! If someone demands your coat, give him your shirt besides. Give what you have to anyone who asks you for it; and when things are taken away from you, don't worry about getting them back. Treat others as you want them to treat you.

"Do you think you deserve credit for merely loving those who love you? Even the godless do that! And if you do good only to those who do you good—is that so wonderful? Even sinners do that much! And if you lend money only to those who can repay you, what good is that? Even the most wicked will lend to their own kind for full return!

"Love your *enemies!* Do good to *them!* Lend to *them!* And don't be concerned about the fact that they won't repay. Then your reward from heaven will be very great, and you will truly be acting as sons of God: for he is kind to the *unthankful* and to those who are *very wicked*.

"Try to show as much compassion as your Father does. Never criticize or condemn—or it will all come back on you. Go easy on others; then they will do the same for you. For if you give, you will get! Your gift will return to you in full and overflowing measure, pressed down, shaken together to make room for more, and running over. Whatever measure you use to give—large or small—will be used to measure what is given back to you."

Here are some of the story-illustrations Jesus used in his sermons: "What good is it for one blind man to lead another? He will fall into a ditch and pull the other down with him. How can a student know more than his teacher? But if he works hard, he may learn as much.

"And why quibble about the speck in someone else's eye—his little fault—when a board is in your own? How can you think of saying to him, 'Brother, let me help you get rid of that speck in your eye,' when you can't see past the board in yours? Hypocrite! First get rid of the board, and then perhaps you can see well enough to deal with his speck!

"A tree from good stock doesn't produce scrub fruit nor do trees from poor stock produce choice fruit. A tree is identified by the kind of fruit it produces. Figs never grow on thorns, or grapes on bramble bushes. A good man produces good deeds from a good heart. And an evil man produces evil deeds from his hidden wickedness. Whatever is in the heart overflows into speech.

"So why do you call me 'Lord' when you won't obey me? But all those who come and listen and obey me are like a man who builds a house on a strong foundation laid upon the underlying rock. When the floodwaters rise and break against the house, it stands firm, for it is strongly built.

"But those who listen and don't obey are like a man who builds a house without a foundation. When the floods sweep down against that house, it crumbles into a heap of ruins."

7

When Jesus had finished his sermon he went back into the city of Capernaum.

Just at that time the highly prized slave of a Roman army captain was sick and near death. When the captain heard about Jesus, he sent some respected Jewish elders to ask him to come and heal his slave. So they began pleading earnestly with Jesus to come with them and help the man. They told him what a wonderful person the captain was.

"If anyone deserves your help, it is he," they said, "for he loves the Jews and even paid personally to build us a synagogue!"

Jesus went with them; but just before arriving at the house, the captain sent some friends to say, "Sir, don't inconvenience yourself by coming to my home, for I am not worthy of any such honor or even to come and meet you. Just speak a word from where you are, and my servant boy will be healed! I know, because I am under the authority of my superior officers, and I have authority over my men. I only need to say 'Go!' and they go; or 'Come!' and they come; and to my slave, 'Do this or that,' and he does it. So just say, 'Be healed!' and my servant will be well again!"

Jesus was amazed. Turning to the crowd he said, "Never among all the Jews in Israel have I met a man with faith like this."

And when the captain's friends returned to his house, they found the slave completely healed.

Not long afterwards Jesus went with his disciples to the village of Nain, with the usual great crowd at his heels. A funeral procession was coming out as he approached the village gate. The boy who had died was the only son of his widowed mother, and many mourners from the village were with her.

When the Lord saw her, his heart overflowed with sympathy. "Don't cry!" he said. Then he walked over to the coffin and touched it, and the bearers stopped. "Laddie," he said, "come back to life again."

Then the boy sat up and began to talk to those around him! And Jesus gave him back to his mother.

A great fear swept the crowd, and they exclaimed with praises to God, "A mighty prophet has risen among us," and, "We have seen the hand of God at work today."

The report of what he did that day raced from end to end of Judea and even out across the borders.

The disciples of John the Baptist soon heard of all that Jesus was doing. When they told John about it, he sent two of his disciples to Jesus to ask him, "Are you really the Messiah? Or shall we keep on looking for him?"

The two disciples found Jesus while he was curing many sick people of their various diseases—healing the lame and the blind and casting out evil spirits. When they asked him John's question, this was his reply: "Go back to John and tell him all you have seen and heard here today: how those who were blind can see. The lame are walking without a limp. The lepers are completely healed. The deaf can hear again. The dead come back to life. And the poor are hearing the Good News. And tell him, 'Blessed is the one who does not lose his faith in me.'"

After they left, Jesus talked to the crowd about John. "Who is this man you went out into the Judean wilderness to see?" he asked. "Did you find him weak as grass, moved by every breath of wind? Did you find him dressed in expensive clothes? No! Men who live in luxury are found in palaces, not out in the wilderness. But did you find a prophet? Yes! And more than a prophet. He is the one to whom the Scriptures refer when they say, 'Look! I am sending my messenger ahead of you, to prepare the way before you.' In all humanity there is no one greater than John. And yet the least citizen of the Kingdom of God is greater than he."

And all who heard John preach—even the most wicked of them—agreed that God's requirements were right, and they were baptized by him. All, that is, except the Pharisees and teachers of Moses' Law. They rejected God's plan for them and refused John's baptism.

"What can I say about such men?" Jesus asked. "With what shall I compare them? They are like a group of children who complain to their friends, 'You don't like it if we play "wedding" and you don't like it if we play "funeral" '! For John the Baptist used to go without food and never took a drop of liquor all his life, and you said, 'He must be crazy!' But I eat my food and drink my wine, and you say, 'What a glutton Jesus is! And he drinks! And has the lowest sort of friends!' But I am sure you can always justify your inconsistencies."

One of the Pharisees asked Jesus to come to his home for lunch and Jesus accepted the invitation. As they sat down to eat, a woman of the streets—a prostitute—heard he was there and brought an cxquisite flask filled with expensive perfume. Going in, she knelt behind him at his feet, weeping, with her tears falling down upon his feet; and she wiped them off with her hair and kissed them and poured the perfume on them.

When Jesus' host, a Pharisee, saw what was happening and who the woman was, he said to himself, "This proves that Jesus is no prophet, for if God had really sent him, he would know what kind of woman this one is!"

Then Jesus spoke up and answered his thoughts. "Simon," he said to the Pharisee, "I have something to say to you."

"All right, Teacher," Simon replied, "go ahead."

Then Jesus told him this story: "A man loaned money to two people—$5,000 to one and $500 to the other. But neither of them could pay him back, so he kindly forgave them both, letting them keep the money! Which do you suppose loved him most after that?"

"I suppose the one who had owed him the most," Simon answered.

"Correct," Jesus agreed.

Then he turned to the woman and said to Simon, "Look! See this woman kneeling here! When I entered your home, you didn't bother to offer me water to wash the dust from my feet, but she has washed them with her tears and wiped them with her hair. You refused me the customary kiss of greeting, but she has kissed my feet again and again from the time I first came in. You neglected the usual courtesy of olive oil to anoint my head, but she has covered my feet with rare perfume. Therefore her sins—and they are many—are forgiven, for she loved me much; but one who is forgiven little, shows little love."

And he said to her, "Your sins are forgiven."

Then the men at the table said to themselves, "Who does this man think he is, going around forgiving sins?"

And Jesus said to the woman, "Your faith has saved you; go in peace."

8

Not long afterwards he began a tour of the cities and villages of Galilee to announce the coming of the Kingdom of God, and took his twelve disciples with him. Some women went along, from whom he had cast out demons or whom he had healed; among them were Mary Magdalene (Jesus had cast out seven demons from her), Joanna, Chuza's wife (Chuza was King Herod's business manager and was in charge of his palace and domestic affairs), Susanna, and many others who were contributing from their private means to the support of Jesus and his disciples.

One day he gave this illustration to a large crowd that was gathering to hear him—while many others were still on the way, coming from other towns.

"A farmer went out to his field to sow grain. As he scattered the seed on the ground, some of it fell on a footpath and was trampled on; and the birds came and ate it as it lay exposed. Other seed fell on shallow soil with rock beneath. This seed began to grow, but soon withered and died for lack of moisture. Other seed landed in thistle patches, and the young grain stalks were soon choked out. Still others fell on fertile soil; this seed grew and produced a crop one hundred times as large as he had planted." (As he was giving this illustration he said, "If anyone has listening ears, use them now!")

His apostles asked him what the story meant.

He replied, "God has granted you to know the meaning of these parables, for they tell a great deal about the Kingdom of God. But these crowds hear the words and do not understand, just as the ancient prophets predicted.

"This is its meaning: The seed is God's message to men. The hard path where some seed fell represents the hard hearts of those who hear the words of God, but then the devil comes and steals the words away and prevents people from believing and being saved. The stony ground represents those who enjoy listening to sermons, but somehow the message never really gets through to them and doesn't take root and grow. They know the message is true, and sort of believe for awhile; but when the hot winds of persecution blow, they lose interest. The seed among the thorns represents those who listen and believe God's words but whose faith afterwards is choked out by worry and riches and the responsibilities and pleasures of life. And so they are never able to help anyone else to believe the Good News.

"But the good soil represents honest, good-hearted people. They listen to God's words and cling to them and steadily spread them to others who also soon believe."

[Another time he asked,] "Who ever heard of someone lighting a lamp and then covering it up to keep it from shining? No, lamps are mounted in the open where they can be seen. This illustrates the fact that someday everything [in men's hearts] shall be brought to light and made plain to all. So be careful how you listen; for whoever has, to him shall be given more; and whoever does not have, even what he thinks he has shall be taken away from him."

Once when his mother and brothers came to see him, they couldn't get into the house where he was teaching, because of the crowds. When Jesus heard they were standing outside and wanted to see him, he remarked, "My mother and my brothers are all those who hear the message of God and obey it."

One day about that time, as he and his disciples were out in a boat, he suggested that they cross to the other side of the lake. On the way across he lay down for a nap, and while he was sleeping the wind began to rise. A fierce storm developed that threatened to swamp them, and they were in real danger.

They rushed over and woke him up. "Master, Master, we are sinking!" they screamed.

So he spoke to the storm: "Quiet down," he said, and the wind and waves subsided and all was calm! Then he asked them, "Where is your faith?"

And they were filled with awe and fear of him and said to one another, "Who is this man, that even the winds and waves obey him?"

So they arrived at the other side, in the Gerasene country across the lake from Galilee. As he was climbing out of the boat a man from the city of Gadara came to meet him, a man who had been demon-possessed for a long time. Homeless and naked, he lived in a cemetery among the tombs. As soon as he saw Jesus he shrieked and fell to the ground before him, screaming, "What do you want with me, Jesus, Son of God Most High? Please, I beg you, oh, don't torment me!"

For Jesus was already commanding the demon to leave him. This demon had often taken control of the man so that even when shackled with chains he simply broke them and rushed out into the desert, completely under the demon's power. "What is your name?" Jesus asked the demon. "Legion," they replied—for the man was filled with thousands of them! They kept begging Jesus not to order them into the Bottomless Pit.

A herd of pigs was feeding on the mountainside nearby, and the demons pled with him to let them enter into the pigs. And Jesus said they could. So they left the man and went into the pigs, and immediately the whole herd rushed down the mountainside and fell over a cliff into the lake below, where they drowned. The herdsmen rushed away to the nearby city, spreading the news as they ran.

Soon a crowd came out to see for themselves what had happened and saw the man who had been demon-possessed sitting quietly at Jesus' feet, clothed and sane! And the whole crowd was badly frightened. Then those who had seen it happen told how the demon-possessed man had been healed. And everyone begged Jesus to go away and leave them alone (for a deep wave of fear had swept over them). So he returned to the boat and left, crossing back to the other side of the lake.

The man who had been demon-possessed begged to go too, but Jesus said no.

"Go back to your family," he told him, "and tell them what a wonderful thing God has done for you."

So he went all through the city telling everyone about Jesus' mighty miracle.

On the other side of the lake the crowds received him with open arms, for they had been waiting for him.

And now a man named Jairus, a leader of a Jewish synagogue, came and fell down at Jesus' feet and begged Jesus to come home with him, for his only child was dying, a little girl twelve years old. Jesus went with him, pushing through the crowds.

As they went a woman who wanted to be healed came up behind and touched him, for she had been slowly bleeding for twelve years, and could find no cure (though she had spent everything she had on doctors). But the instant she touched the edge of his robe, the bleeding stopped.

"Who touched me?" Jesus asked.

Everyone denied it, and Peter said, "Master, so many are crowding against you. . . ."

But Jesus told him, "No, it was someone who deliberately touched me, for I felt healing power go out from me."

When the woman realized that Jesus knew, she began to tremble and fell to her knees before him and told why she had touched him and that now she was well.

"Daughter," he said to her, "your faith has healed you. Go in peace."

While he was still speaking to her, a messenger arrived from the Jairus' home with the news that the little girl was dead. "She's gone," he told her father; "there's no use troubling the Teacher now."

But when Jesus heard what had happened, he said to the father, "Don't be afraid! Just trust me, and she'll be all right."

When they arrived at the house Jesus wouldn't let anyone into the room except Peter, James, John, and the little girl's father and mother. The home was filled with mourning people, but he said,

"Stop the weeping! She isn't dead; she is only asleep!" This brought scoffing and laughter, for they all knew she was dead.

Then he took her by the hand and called, "Get up, little girl!" And at that moment her life returned and she jumped up! "Give her something to eat!" he said. Her parents were overcome with happiness, but Jesus insisted that they not tell anyone the details of what had happened.

9

One day Jesus called together his twelve apostles and gave them authority over all demons—power to cast them out—and to heal all diseases. Then he sent them away to tell everyone about the coming of the Kingdom of God and to heal the sick.

"Don't even take along a walking stick," he instructed them, "nor a beggar's bag, nor food, nor money. Not even an extra coat. Be a guest in only one home at each village.

"If the people of a town won't listen to you when you enter it, turn around and leave, demonstrating God's anger against it by shaking its dust from your feet as you go."

So they began their circuit of the villages, preaching the Good News and healing the sick.

When reports of Jesus' miracles reached Herod, the governor, he was worried and puzzled, for some were saying, "This is John the Baptist come back to life again"; and others, "It is Elijah or some other ancient prophet risen from the dead." These rumors were circulating all over the land.

"I beheaded John," Herod said, "so who is this man about whom I hear such strange stories?" And he tried to see him.

After the apostles returned to Jesus and reported what they had done, he slipped quietly away with them toward the city of Bethsaida. But the crowds found out where he was going, and followed. And he welcomed them, teaching them again about the Kingdom of God and curing those who were ill.

Late in the afternoon all twelve of the disciples came and urged him to send the people away to the nearby villages and farms, to find food and lodging for the night. "For there is nothing to eat here in this deserted spot," they said.

But Jesus replied, "*You* feed them!"

"Why, we have only five loaves of bread and two fish among the lot of us," they protested; "or are you expecting us to go and buy enough for this whole mob?" For there were about 5,000 men there!

"Just tell them to sit down on the ground in groups of about fifty each," Jesus replied. So they did.

Jesus took the five loaves and two fish and looked up into the sky and gave thanks; then he broke off pieces for his disciples to set before the crowd. And everyone ate and ate; still, twelve basketfuls of scraps were picked up afterwards!

One day as he was alone, praying, with his disciples nearby, he came over and asked them, "Who are the people saying I am?"

"John the Baptist," they told him, "or perhaps Elijah or one of the other ancient prophets risen from the dead."

Then he asked them, "Who do you think I am?"

Peter replied, "The Messiah—the Christ of God!"

He gave them strict orders not to speak of this to anyone. "For I, the Messiah, must suffer much," he said, "and be rejected by the Jewish leaders—the elders, chief priests, and teachers of the Law—and be killed; and three days later I will come back to life again!"

Then he said to all, "Anyone who wants to follow me must put aside his own desires and conveniences and carry his cross with him every day and *keep close to me!* Whoever loses his life for my sake will save it, but whoever insists on keeping his life will lose it; and what profit is there in gaining the whole world when it means forfeiting one's self?

"When I, the Messiah, come in my glory and in the glory of the Father and the holy angels, I will be ashamed then of all who are ashamed of me and of my words now. But this is the simple truth—some of you who are standing here right now will not die until you have seen the Kingdom of God."

Eight days later he took Peter, James, and John with him into the hills to pray. And as he was praying, his face began to shine, and his clothes became dazzling white and blazed with light. Then two men appeared and began talking with him—Moses and Elijah! They were splendid in appearance, glorious to see; and they were speaking of his death at Jerusalem, to be carried out in accordance with God's plan.

Peter and the others had been very drowsy and had fallen asleep. Now they woke up and saw Jesus covered with brightness and glory, and the two men standing with him. As Moses and Elijah were starting to leave, Peter, all confused and not even knowing what he was saying, blurted out, "Master, this is wonderful! We'll put up three shelters—one for you and one for Moses and one for Elijah!"

But even as he was saying this, a bright cloud formed above them; and terror gripped them as it covered them. And a voice from the cloud said, "*This* is my Son, my Chosen One; listen to *him.*"

Then, as the voice died away, Jesus was there alone with his disciples. They didn't tell anyone what they had seen until long afterwards.

The next day as they descended from the hill, a huge crowd met him, and a man in the crowd called out to him, "Teacher, this boy here is my only son, and a demon keeps seizing him, making him scream; and it throws him into convulsions so that he foams at the mouth; it is always hitting him and hardly ever leaves him alone. I begged your disciples to cast the demon out, but they couldn't."

"O you stubborn faithless people," Jesus said [to his disciples], "how long should I put up with you? Bring him here."

As the boy was coming the demon knocked him to the ground and threw him into a violent convulsion. But Jesus ordered the demon to come out, and healed the boy and handed him over to his father.

Awe gripped the people as they saw this display of the power of God.

Meanwhile, as they were exclaiming over all the wonderful things he was doing, Jesus said to his disciples, "Listen to me and remember what I say. I, the Messiah, am going to be betrayed." But the disciples didn't know what he meant, for their minds had been sealed and they were afraid to ask him.

Now came an argument among them as to which of them would be greatest [in the coming Kingdom]! But Jesus knew their thoughts, so he stood a little child beside him and said to them, "Anyone who takes care of a little child like this is caring for me! And whoever cares for me is caring for God who sent me. Your care for others is the measure of your greatness." His disciple John came to him and said, "Master, we saw someone using your name to cast out demons. And we told him not to. After all, he isn't in our group."

But Jesus said, "You shouldn't have done that! For anyone who is not against you is for you."

As the time drew near for his return to heaven, he moved steadily onward towards Jerusalem with an iron will.

One day he sent messengers ahead to reserve rooms for them in a Samaritan village. But they were turned away! The people of the village refused to have anything to do with them because they were headed for Jerusalem.

When word came back of what had happened, James and John said to Jesus, "Master, shall we order fire down from heaven to burn them up?" But Jesus turned and rebuked them, and they went on to another village.

As they were walking along someone said to Jesus, "I will always follow you no matter where you go."

But Jesus replied, "Remember, I don't even own a place to lay my head. Foxes have dens to live in, and birds have nests, but I, the Messiah, have no earthly home at all."

Another time, when he invited a man to come with him and to be his disciple, the man agreed—but wanted to wait until his father's death.

Jesus replied, "Let those without eternal life concern themselves with things like that. Your duty is to come and preach the coming of the Kingdom of God to all the world."

Another said, "Yes, Lord, I will come, but first let me ask permission of those at home."

But Jesus told him, "Anyone who lets himself be distracted from the work I plan for him is not fit for the Kingdom of God."

10

The Lord now chose seventy other disciples and sent them on ahead in pairs to all the towns and villages he planned to visit later.

These were his instructions to them: "Plead with the Lord of the harvest to send out more laborers to help you, for the harvest is so plentiful and the workers so few. Go now, and remember that I am sending you out as lambs among wolves. Don't take any money with you, or a beggar's bag, or even an extra pair of shoes. And don't waste time along the way.

"Whenever you enter a home, give it your blessing. If it is worthy of the blessing, the blessing will stand; if not, the blessing will return to you.

"When you enter a village, don't shift around from home to home, but stay in one place, eating and drinking without question whatever is set before you. And don't hesitate to accept hospitality, for the workman is worthy of his wages!

"If a town welcomes you, follow these two rules:

(1) Eat whatever is set before you.

(2) Heal the sick; and as you heal them, say, 'The Kingdom of God is very near you now.'

"But if a town refuses you, go out into its streets and say, 'We wipe the dust of your town from out feet as a public announcement of your doom. Never forget how close you were to the Kingdom of God!' Even wicked Sodom will be better off than such a city on the Judgment Day. What horrors await you, you cities of Chorazin and Bethsaida! For if the miracles I did for you had been done in the cities of Tyre and Sidon, their people would have sat in deep repentance long ago, clothed in sackcloth and throwing ashes on their heads to show their remorse. Yes, Tyre and Sidon will receive less punishment on the Judgment Day than you. And you people of Capernaum, what shall I say about you? Will you be exalted to heaven? No, you shall be brought down to hell."

Then he said to the disciples, "Those who welcome you are welcoming me. And those who reject you are rejecting me. And those who reject me are rejecting God who sent me."

When the seventy disciples returned, they joyfully reported to him, "Even the demons obey us when we use your name."

"Yes," he told them, "I saw Satan falling from heaven as a flash of lightning! And I have given you authority over all the power of the Enemy, and to walk among serpents and scorpions and to crush them. Nothing shall injure you! However, the important thing is not that demons obey you, but that your names are registered as citizens of heaven."

Then he was filled with the joy of the Holy Spirit and said, "I praise you, O Father, Lord of heaven and earth, for hiding these things from the intellectuals and worldly wise and for revealing them to those who are as trusting as little children. Yes, thank you, Father, for that is the way you wanted it. I am the Agent of my Father in everything; and no one really knows the Son except the Father, and no one really knows the Father except the Son and those to whom the Son chooses to reveal him."

Then, turning to the twelve disciples, he said quietly, "How privileged you are to see what you have seen. Many a prophet and king of old has longed for these days, to see and hear what you have seen and heard!"

One day an expert on Moses' laws came to test Jesus' orthodoxy by asking him this question: "Teacher, what does a man need to do to live forever in heaven?"

Jesus replied, "What does Moses' law say about it?"

"It says," he replied, "that you must love the Lord your God with all your heart, and with all your soul, and with all your strength, and with all your mind. And you must love your neighbor just as much as you love yourself."

"Right!" Jesus told him. "*Do* this and *you* shall live!"

The man wanted to justify (his lack of love for some kinds of people), so he asked, "Which neighbors?"

Jesus replied with an illustration: "A Jew going on a trip from Jerusalem to Jericho was attacked by bandits. They stripped him of his clothes and money and beat him up and left him lying half dead beside the road.

"By chance a Jewish priest came along; and when he saw the man lying there, he crossed to the other side of the road and passed him by. A Jewish Temple-assistant walked over and looked at him lying there, but then went on.

"But a despised Samaritan came along, and when he saw him, he felt deep pity. Kneeling beside him the Samaritan soothed his wounds with medicine and bandaged them. Then he put the man on his donkey and walked along beside him till they came to an inn, where he nursed him through the night. The next day he handed the innkeeper two twenty-dollar bills and told him to take care of the man. 'If his bill runs higher than that,' he said, 'I'll pay the difference the next time I am here.'

"Now which of these three would you say was a neighbor to the bandits' victim?"

The man replied, "The one who showed him some pity."

Then Jesus said, "Yes, now go and do the same."

As Jesus and the disciples continued on their way to Jerusalem they came to a village where a woman named Martha welcomed them into her home. Her sister Mary sat on the floor, listening to Jesus as he talked.

But Martha was the jittery type, and was worrying over the big dinner she was preparing.

She came to Jesus and said, "Sir, doesn't it seem unfair to you that my sister just sits here while I do all the work? Tell her to come and help me."

But the Lord said to her, "Martha, dear friend, you are so upset over all these details! There is really only one thing worth being concerned about. Mary has discovered it—and I won't take it away from her!"

11

Once when Jesus had been out praying, one of his disciples came to him as he finished and said, "Lord, teach us a prayer to recite just as John taught one to his disciples."

And this is the prayer he taught them: "Father, may your name be honored for its holiness; send your Kingdom soon. Give us our food day by day. And forgive our sins—for we have forgiven those who sinned against us. And don't allow us to be tempted."

Then, teaching them more about prayer, he used this illustration: "Suppose you went to a friend's house at midnight, wanting to borrow three loaves of bread. You would shout up to him, 'A friend of mine has just arrived for a visit and I've nothing to give him to eat.' He would call down from his bedroom, 'Please don't ask me to get up. The door is locked for the night and we are all in bed. I just can't help you this time.'

"But I'll tell you this—though he won't do it as a friend, if you keep knocking long enough he will get up and give you everything you want—just because of your persistence. And so it is with prayer—keep on looking and you will keep on finding; knock and the door will be opened. Everyone who asks, receives; all who seek, find; and the door is opened to everyone who knocks.

"You men who are fathers—if your boy asks for bread, do you give him a stone? If he asks for fish, do you give him a snake? If he asks for an egg, do you give him a scorpion? [Of course not!]

"And if even sinful persons like yourselves give children what they need, don't you realize that your heavenly Father will do at least as much, and give the Holy Spirit to those who ask for him?"

Once, when Jesus cast out a demon from a man who couldn't speak, his voice returned to him. The crowd was excited and enthusiastic, but some said, "No wonder he can cast them out. He gets his power from Satan, the king of demons!" Others asked for something to happen in the sky to prove his claim of being the Messiah.

He knew the thoughts of each of them, so he said, "Any kingdom filled with civil war is doomed; so is a home filled with argument and strife. Therefore, if what you say is true, that Satan is fighting against himself by empowering me to cast out his demons, how can his kingdom survive? And if I am empowered by Satan, what about your own followers? For they cast out demons! Do you think this proves they are possessed by Satan? Ask *them* if you are right! But if I am casting out demons because of power from God, it proves that the Kingdom of God has arrived.

"For when Satan, strong and fully armed, guards his palace, it is safe—until someone stronger and better-armed attacks and overcomes him and strips him of his weapons and carries off his belongings.

"Anyone who is not for me is against me; if he isn't helping me, he is hurting my cause.

"When a demon is cast out of a man, it goes to the deserts, searching there for rest; but finding none, it returns to the person it left, and finds that its former home is all swept and clean. Then it goes and gets seven other demons more evil than itself, and they all enter the man. And so the poor fellow is seven times worse off than he was before."

As he was speaking, a woman in the crowd called out, "God bless your mother—the womb from which you came, and the breasts that gave you suck!"

He replied, "Yes, but even more blessed are all who hear the Word of God and put it into practice."

As the crowd pressed in upon him, he preached them this sermon: "These are evil times, with evil people. They keep asking for some strange happening in the skies [to prove I am the Messiah], but the only proof I will give them is a miracle like that of Jonah, whose experiences proved to the people of Nineveh that God had sent him. My similar experience will prove that God has sent me to these people.

"And at the Judgment Day the Queen of Sheba shall arise and point her finger at this generation, condemning it, for she went on a long, hard journey to listen to the wisdom of Solomon; but one far greater than Solomon is here [and few pay any attention].

"The men of Nineveh, too, shall arise and condemn this nation, for they repented at the preaching of Jonah; and someone far greater than Jonah is here [but this nation won't listen].

"No one lights a lamp and hides it! Instead, he puts it on a lampstand to give light to all who enter the room. Your eyes light up your inward being. A pure eye lets sunshine into your soul. A lustful eye shuts out the light and plunges you into darkness. So watch out that the sunshine isn't blotted out. If you are filled with light within, with no dark corners, then your face will be radiant too, as though a floodlight is beamed upon you."

As he was speaking, one of the Pharisees asked him home for a meal. When Jesus arrived, he sat down to eat without first performing the ceremonial washing required by Jewish custom. This greatly surprised his host.

Then Jesus said to him, "You Pharisees wash the outside, but inside you are still dirty—full of greed and wickedness! Fools! Didn't God make the inside as well as the outside? Purity is best demonstrated by generosity.

"But woe to you Pharisees! For though you are careful to tithe even the smallest part of your income, you completely forget about justice and the love of God. You should tithe, yes, but you should not leave these other things undone.

"Woe to you Pharisees! For how you love the seats of honor in the synagogues and the respectful greetings from everyone as you walk through the markets! Yes, awesome judgment is awaiting you. For you are like hidden graves in a field. Men go by you with no knowledge of the corruption they are passing."

"Sir," said an expert in religious law who was standing there, "you have insulted my profession, too, in what you just said."

"Yes," said Jesus, "the same horrors await you! For you crush men beneath impossible religious demands—demands that you yourselves would never think of trying to keep. Woe to you! For you are exactly like your ancestors who killed the prophets long ago. Murderers! You agree with your fathers that what they did was right—you would have done the same yourselves.

"This is what God says about you: 'I will send prophets and apostles to you, and you will kill some of them and chase away the others.'

"And you of this generation will be held responsible for the murder of God's servants from the founding of the world—from the murder of Abel to the murder of Zechariah who perished between the altar and the sanctuary. Yes, it will surely be charged against you.

"Woe to you experts in religion! For you hide the truth from the people. You won't accept it for yourselves, and you prevent others from having a chance to believe it."

The Pharisees and legal experts were furious; and from that time on they plied him fiercely with a host of questions, trying to trap him into saying something for which they could have him arrested.

12

Meanwhile the crowds grew until thousands upon thousands were milling about and crushing each other. He turned now to his disciples and warned them, "More than anything else, beware of these Pharisees and the way they pretend to be good when they aren't. But such hypocrisy cannot be hidden forever. It will become as evident as yeast in dough. Whatever they have said in the dark shall be heard in the light, and what you have whispered in the inner rooms shall be broadcast from the housetops for all to hear!

"Dear friends, don't be afraid of these who want to murder you. They can only kill the body; they have no power over your souls. But I'll tell you whom to fear—fear God who has the power to kill and then cast into hell.

"What is the price of five sparrows? A couple of pennies? Not much more than that. Yet God does not forget a single one of them. And he knows the number of hairs on your head! Never fear, you are far more valuable to him than a whole flock of sparrows.

"And I assure you of this: I, the Messiah, will publicly honor you in the presence of God's angels if you publicly acknowledge me here on earth as your Friend. But I will deny before the angels those who deny me here among men. (Yet those who speak against me may be forgiven—while those who speak against the Holy Spirit shall never be forgiven.)

"And when you are brought to trial before these Jewish rulers and authorities in the synagogues, don't be concerned about what to say in your defense, for the Holy Spirit will give you the right words even as you are standing there."

Then someone called from the crowd, "Sir, please tell my brother to divide my father's estate with me."

But Jesus replied, "Man, who made me a judge over you to decide such things as that? Beware! Don't always be wishing for what you don't have. For real life and real living are not related to how rich we are."

Then he gave an illustration: "A rich man had a fertile farm that produced fine crops. In fact, his barns were full to overflowing—he couldn't get everything in. He thought about his problem, and finally exclaimed, 'I know—I'll tear down my barns and build bigger ones! Then I'll have room enough. And I'll sit back and say to myself, "Friend, you have enough stored away for years to come. Now take it easy! Wine, women, and song for you!" '

"But God said to him, 'Fool! Tonight you die. Then who will get it all?'

"Yes, every man is a fool who gets rich on earth but not in heaven."

Then turning to his disciples he said, "Don't worry about whether you have enough food to eat or clothes to wear. For life consists of far more than food and clothes. Look at the ravens—they don't plant or harvest or have barns to store away their food, and yet they get along all right—for God feeds them. And you are far more valuable to him than any birds!

"And besides, what's the use of worrying? What good does it do? Will it add a single day to your life? Of course not! And if worry can't even do such little things as that, what's the use of worrying over bigger things?

"Look at the lilies! They don't toil and spin, and yet Solomon in all his glory was not robed as well as they are. And if God provides clothing for the flowers that are here today and gone tomorrow, don't you suppose that he will provide clothing for you, you doubters? And don't worry about food—what to eat and drink; don't worry at all that God will provide it for you. All mankind scratches for its daily bread, but your heavenly Father knows your needs. He will always give you all you need from day to day if you will make the Kingdom of God your primary concern.

"So don't be afraid, little flock. For it gives your Father great happiness to give you the Kingdom. Sell what you have and give to those in need. This will fatten your purses in heaven! And the purses of heaven have no rips or holes in them. Your treasures there will never disappear; no thief can steal them; no moth can destroy them. Wherever your treasure is, there your heart and thoughts will also be.

"Be prepared—all dressed and ready—for your Lord's return from the wedding feast. Then you will be ready to open the door and let him in the moment he arrives and knocks. There will be great joy for those who are ready and waiting for his return. He himself will seat them and put on a waiter's uniform and serve them as they sit and eat! He may come at nine o'clock at night—or even at midnight. But whenever he comes there will be joy for his servants who are ready!

"Everyone would be ready for him if they knew the exact hour of his return—just as they would be ready for a thief if they knew when he was coming. So be ready all the time. For I, the Messiah, will come when least expected."

Peter asked, "Lord, are you talking just to us or to everyone?"

And the Lord replied, "I'm talking to any faithful, sensible man whose master gives him the responsibility of feeding the other servants. If his master returns and finds that he has done a good job, there will be a reward—his master will put him in charge of all he owns.

"But if the man begins to think, 'My Lord won't be back for a long time,' and begins to whip the men and women he is supposed to protect, and to spend his time at drinking parties and in drunkenness—well, his master will return without notice and remove him from his position of trust and assign him to the place of the unfaithful. He will be severely punished, for though he knew his duty he refused to do it.

"But anyone who is not aware that he is doing wrong will be punished only lightly. Much is required from those to whom much is given, for their responsibility is greater.

"I have come to bring fire to the earth, and, oh, that my task were completed! There is a terrible baptism ahead of me, and how I am pent up until it is accomplished!

"Do you think I have come to give peace to the earth? *No!* Rather, strife and division! From now on families will be split apart, three in favor of me, and two against—or perhaps the other way around. A father will decide one way about me; his son, the other; mother and daughter will disagree; and the decision of an honored mother-in-law will be spurned by her daughter-in-law."

Then he turned to the crowd and said, "When you see clouds beginning to form in the west, you say, 'Here comes a shower.' And you are right.

"When the south wind blows you say, 'Today will be a scorcher.' And it is. Hypocrites! You interpret the sky well enough, but you refuse to notice the warnings all around you about the crisis ahead. Why do you refuse to see for yourselves what is right?

"If you meet your accuser on the way to court, try to settle the matter before it reaches the judge, lest he sentence you to jail; for if that happens you won't be free again until the last penny is paid in full."

13

About this time he was informed that Pilate had butchered some Jews from Galilee as they were sacrificing at the Temple in Jerusalem.

"Do you think they were worse sinners than other men from Galilee?" he asked. "Is that why they suffered? Not at all! And don't you realize that you also will perish unless you leave your evil ways and turn to God?

"And what about the eighteen men who died when the Tower of Siloam fell on them? Were they the worst sinners in Jerusalem? Not at all! And you, too, will perish unless you repent."

Then he used this illustration: "A man planted a fig tree in his garden and came again and again to see if he could find any fruit on it, but he was always disappointed. Finally he told his gardener to cut it down. 'I've waited three years and there hasn't been a single fig!' he said. 'Why bother with it any longer? It's taking up space we can use for something else.'

" 'Give it one more chance,' the gardener answered. 'Leave it another year, and I'll give it special attention and plenty of fertilizer. If we get figs next year, fine; if not, I'll cut it down.' "

One Sabbath as he was teaching in a synagogue, he saw a seriously handicapped woman who had been bent double for eighteen years and was unable to straighten herself.

Calling her over to him Jesus said, "Woman, you are healed of your sickness!" He touched her, and instantly she could stand straight. How she praised and thanked God!

But the local Jewish leader in charge of the synagogue was very angry about it because Jesus had healed her on the Sabbath day. "There are six days of the week to work," he shouted to the crowd. "Those are the days to come for healing, not on the Sabbath!"

But the Lord replied, "You hypocrite! You work on the Sabbath! Don't you untie your cattle from their stalls on the Sabbath and lead them out for water? And is it wrong for me, just because it is the Sabbath day, to free this Jewish woman from the bondage in which Satan has held her for eighteen years?"

This shamed his enemies. And all the people rejoiced at the wonderful things he did.

Now he began teaching them again about the Kingdom of God: "What is the Kingdom like?" he asked. "How can I illustrate it? It is like a tiny mustard seed planted in a garden; soon it grows into a tall bush and the birds live among its branches.

It is like yeast kneaded into dough, which works unseen until it has risen high and light."

He went from city to city and village to village, teaching as he went, always pressing onward toward Jerusalem.

Someone asked him, "Will only a few be saved?"

And he replied, "The door to heaven is narrow. Work hard to get in, for the truth is that many will try to enter but when the head of the house has locked the door, it will be too late. Then if you stand outside knocking, and pleading, 'Lord, open the door for us,' he will reply, 'I do not know you.'

" 'But we ate with you, and you taught in our streets,' you will say.

"And he will reply, 'I tell you, I don't know you. You can't come in here, guilty as you are. Go away.'

"And there will be great weeping and gnashing of teeth as you stand outside and see Abraham, Isaac, Jacob, and all the prophets within the Kingdom of God—for people will come from all over the world to take their places there. And note this: some who are despised now will be greatly honored then; and some who are highly thought of now will be least important then."

A few minutes later some Pharisees said to him, "Get out of here if you want to live, for King Herod is after you!"

Jesus replied, "Go tell that fox that I will keep on casting out demons and doing miracles of healing today and tomorrow; and the third day I will reach my destination. Yes, today, tomorrow, and the next day! For it wouldn't do for a prophet of God to be killed except in Jerusalem!

"O Jerusalem, Jerusalem! The city that murders the prophets. The city that stones those sent to help her. How often I have wanted to gather your children together even as a hen protects her brood under her wings, but you wouldn't let me. And now—now your house is left desolate. And you will never again see me until you say, 'Welcome to him who comes in the name of the Lord.' "

14

One Sabbath as he was in the home of a member of the Jewish Council, the Pharisees were watching him like hawks to see if he would heal a man who was present who was suffering from dropsy.

Jesus said to the Pharisees and legal experts standing around, "Well, is it within the Law to heal a man on the Sabbath day, or not?"

And when they refused to answer, Jesus took the sick man by the hand and healed him and sent him away.

Then he turned to them: "Which of you doesn't work on the Sabbath?" he asked. "If your cow falls into a pit, don't you proceed at once to get it out?"

Again they had no answer.

When he noticed that all who came to the dinner were trying to sit near the head of the table, he gave them this advice: "If you are invited to a wedding feast, don't always head for the best seat. For if someone more respected than you shows up, the host will bring him over to where you are sitting and say, 'Let this man sit here instead.' And you, embarrassed, will have to take whatever seat is left at the foot of the table!

"Do this instead—start at the foot; and when your host sees you he will come and say, 'Friend, we have a better place than this for you!' Thus you will be honored in front of all the other guests. For everyone who tries to honor himself shall be humbled; and he who humbles himself shall be honored." Then he turned to his host. "When you put on a dinner," he said, "don't invite friends, brothers, relatives, and rich neighbors! For they will return the invitation. Instead, invite the poor, the crippled, the lame, and the blind. Then at the resurrection of the godly, God will reward you for inviting those who can't repay you."

Hearing this, a man sitting at the table with Jesus exclaimed, "What a privilege it would be to get into the Kingdom of God!"

Jesus replied with this illustration: "A man prepared a great feast and sent out many invitations. When all was ready, he sent his servant around to notify the guests that it was time for them to arrive. But they all began making excuses. One said he had just bought a field and wanted to inspect it, and asked to be excused. Another said he had just bought five pair of oxen and wanted to try them out. Another had just been married and for that reason couldn't come.

"The servant returned and reported to his master what they had said. His master was angry and told him to go quickly into the streets and alleys of the city and to invite the beggars, crippled, lame, and blind. But even then, there was still room.

" 'Well, then,' said his master, 'go out into the country lanes and out behind the hedges and urge anyone you find to come, so that the house will be full. For none of those I invited first will get even the smallest taste of what I had prepared for them.' "

Great crowds were following him. He turned around and addressed them as follows: "Anyone who wants to be my follower must love me far more than he does his own father, mother, wife, children, brothers, or sisters—yes, more than his own life—otherwise he cannot be my disciple. And no one can be my disciple who does not carry his own cross and follow me.

"But don't begin until you count the cost. For who would begin construction of a building without first getting estimates and then checking to see if he has enough money to pay the bills? Otherwise he might complete only the foundation before running out of funds. And then how everyone would laugh!

" 'See that fellow there?' they would mock. 'He started that building and ran out of money before it was finished!'

"Or what king would ever dream of going to war without first sitting down with his counselors and discussing whether his army of 10,000 is strong enough to defeat the 20,000 men who are marching against him?

"If the decision is negative, then while the enemy troops are still far away, he will send a truce team to discuss terms of peace. So no one can become my disciple unless he first sits down and counts his blessings—and then renounces them all for me.

"What good is salt that has lost its saltiness? Flavorless salt is fit for nothing—not even for fertilizer. It is worthless and must be thrown out. Listen well, if you would understand my meaning."

15

Dishonest tax collectors and other notorious sinners often came to listen to Jesus' sermons; but this caused complaints from the Jewish religious leaders and the experts on Jewish law because he was associating with such despicable people—even eating with them!

So Jesus used this illustration: "If you had a hundred sheep and one of them strayed away and was lost in the wilderness, wouldn't you leave the ninety-nine others to go and search for the lost one until you found it? And then you would joyfully carry it home on your shoulders. When you arrived you would call together your friends and neighbors to rejoice with you because your lost sheep was found.

"Well, in the same way heaven will be happier over one lost sinner who returns to God than over ninety-nine others who haven't strayed away!

"Or take another illustration: A woman has ten valuable silver coins and loses one. Won't she light a lamp and look in every corner of the house and sweep every nook and cranny until she finds it? And then won't she call in her friends and neighbors to rejoice with her? In the same way there is joy in the presence of the angels of God when one sinner repents."

To further illustrate the point, he told them this story: "A man had two sons. When the younger told his father, 'I want my share of your estate now, instead of waiting until you die!' his father agreed to divide his wealth between his sons.

"A few days later this younger son packed all his belongings and took a trip to a distant land, and there wasted all his money on parties and prostitutes. About the time his money was gone a great famine swept over the land, and he began to starve. He persuaded a local farmer to hire him to feed his pigs. The boy became so hungry that even the pods he was feeding the swine looked good to him. And no one gave him anything.

"When he finally came to his senses, he said to himself, 'At home even the hired men have food enough and to spare, and here I am, dying of hunger! I will go home to my father and say, "Father, I have sinned against both heaven and you, and am no longer worthy of being called your son. Please take me on as a hired man." '

"So he returned home to his father. And while he was still a long distance away, his father saw him coming, and was filled with loving pity and ran and embraced him and kissed him.

"His son said to him, 'Father, I have sinned against heaven and you, and am not worthy of being called your son—'

"But his father said to the slaves, "Quick! Bring the finest robe in the house and put it on him. And a jeweled ring for his finger; and shoes! And kill the calf we have in the fattening pen. We must celebrate with a feast, for this son of mine was dead and has returned to life. He was lost and is found.' So the party began.

"Meanwhile, the older son was in the fields working; when he returned home, he heard dance music coming from the house, and he asked one of the servants what was going on.

" 'Your brother is back,' he was told, 'and your father has killed the calf we were fattening and has prepared a great feast to celebrate his coming home again unharmed.'

"The older brother was angry and wouldn't go in. His father came out and begged him, but he replied, 'All these years I've worked hard for you and never once refused to do a single thing you told me to; and in all that time you never gave me even one young goat for a feast with my friends. Yet when this son of yours comes back after spending your money on prostitutes, you celebrate by killing the finest calf we have on the place.'

" 'Look, dear son,' his father said to him, 'you and I are very close, and everything I have is yours. But it is right to celebrate. For he is your brother; and he was dead and has come back to life! He was lost and is found!' "

16

Jesus now told this story to his disciples: "A rich man hired an accountant to handle his affairs, but soon a rumor went around that the accountant was thoroughly dishonest.

"So his employer called him in and said, 'What's this I hear about your stealing from me? Get your report in order, for you are to be dismissed.'

"The accountant thought to himself, 'Now what? I'm through here, and I haven't the strength to go out and dig ditches, and I'm too proud to beg. I know just the thing! And then I'll have plenty of friends to take care of me when I leave!'

"So he invited each one who owed money to his employer to come and discuss the situation. He asked the first one, 'How much do you owe him?' 'My debt is 850 gallons of olive oil,' the man replied. 'Yes, here is the contract you signed,' the accountant told him. 'Tear it up and write another one for half that much!'

" 'And how much do you owe him?' he asked the next man. 'A thousand bushels of wheat,' was the reply. 'Here,' the accountant said, 'take your note and replace it with one for only 800 bushels!'

"The rich man had to admire the rascal for being so shrewd. And it is true that the citizens of this world are more clever [in dishonesty!] than the godly are. But shall I tell *you* to act that way, to buy friendship through cheating? Will this ensure your entry into an everlasting home in heaven? *No!* For unless you are honest in small matters, you won't be in large ones. If you cheat even a little, you won't be honest with greater responsibilities. And if you are untrustworthy about worldly wealth, who will trust you with the true riches of heaven? And if you are not faithful with other people's money, why should you be entrusted with money of your own?

"For neither you nor anyone else can serve two masters. You will hate one and show loyalty to the other, or else the other way around—you will be enthusiastic about one and despise the other. You cannot serve both God and money."

The Pharisees, who dearly loved their money, naturally scoffed at all this.

Then he said to them, "You wear a noble, pious expression in public, but God knows your evil hearts. Your pretense brings you honor from the people, but it is an abomination in the sight of God. Until John the Baptist began to preach, the laws of Moses and the messages of the prophets were your guides. But John introduced the Good News that the Kingdom of God would come soon. And now eager multitudes are pressing in. But that doesn't mean that the Law has lost its force in even the smallest point. It is as strong and unshakable as heaven and earth.

"So anyone who divorces his wife and marries someone else commits adultery, and anyone who marries a divorced woman commits adultery."

"There was a certain rich man," Jesus said, "who was splendidly clothed and lived each day in mirth and luxury. One day Lazarus, a diseased beggar, was laid at his door. As he lay there longing for scraps from the rich man's table, the dogs would come and lick his open sores. Finally the beggar died and was carried by the angels to be with Abraham in the place of the righteous dead. The rich man also died and was buried, and his soul went into hell. There, in torment, he saw Lazarus in the far distance with Abraham.

" 'Father Abraham,' he shouted, 'have some pity! Send Lazarus over here if only to dip the tip of his finger in water and cool my tongue, for I am in anguish in these flames.'

"But Abraham said to him, 'Son, remember that during your lifetime you had everything you wanted, and Lazarus had nothing.

So now he is here being comforted and you are in anguish. And besides, there is a great chasm separating us, and anyone wanting to come to you from here is stopped at its edge; and no one over there can cross to us.'

"Then the rich man said, 'O Father Abraham, then please send him to my father's home—for I have five brothers—to warn them about this place of torment lest they come here when they die.'

"But Abraham said, 'The Scriptures have warned them again and again. Your brothers can read them any time they want to.'

"The rich man replied, 'No, Father Abraham, they won't bother to read them. But if someone is sent to them from the dead, then they will turn from their sins.'

"But Abraham said, 'If they won't listen to Moses and the prophets, they won't listen even though someone rises from the dead.' "

17

There will always be temptations to sin," Jesus said one day to his disciples, "but woe to the man who does the tempting. If he were thrown into the sea with a huge rock tied to his neck, he would be far better off than facing the punishment in store for those who harm these little children's souls. I am warning you!

"Rebuke your brother if he sins, and forgive him if he is sorry. Even if he wrongs you seven times a day and each time turns again and asks forgiveness, forgive him."

One day the apostles said to the Lord, "We need more faith; tell us how to get it."

"If your faith were only the size of a mustard seed," Jesus answered, "it would be large enough to uproot that mulberry tree over there and send it hurtling into the sea! Your command would bring immediate results! When a servant comes in from plowing or taking care of sheep, he doesn't just sit down and eat, but first prepares his master's meal and serves him his supper before he eats his own. And he is not even thanked, for he is merely doing what he is supposed to do. Just so, if you merely obey me, you should not consider yourselves worthy of praise. For you have simply done your duty!"

As they continued onward toward Jerusalem, they reached the border between Galilee and Samaria, and as they entered a village there, ten lepers stood at a distance, crying out, "Jesus, sir, have mercy on us!"

He looked at them and said, "Go to the Jewish priest and show him that you are healed!" And as they were going, their leprosy disappeared.

One of them came back to Jesus, shouting, "Glory to God, I'm healed!" He fell flat on the ground in front of Jesus, face downward in the dust, thanking him for what he had done. This man was a despised Samaritan.

Jesus asked, "Didn't I heal ten men? Where are the nine? Does only this foreigner return to give glory to God?"

And Jesus said to the man, "Stand up and go; your faith has made you well."

One day the Pharisees asked Jesus, "When will the Kingdom of God begin?" Jesus replied, "The Kingdom of God isn't ushered in with visible signs. You won't be able to say, 'It has begun here in this place or there in that part of the country.' For the Kingdom of God is within you."

Later he talked again about this with his disciples. "The time is coming when you will long for me to be with you even for a single day, but I won't be here," he said. "Reports will reach you that I have returned and that I am in this place or that; don't believe it or go out to look for me. For when I return, you will know it beyond all doubt. It will be as evident as the lightning that flashes across the skies. But first I must suffer terribly and be rejected by this whole nation.

"[When I return] the world will be [as indifferent to the things of God] as the people were in Noah's day. They ate and drank and married—everything just as usual right up to the day when Noah went into the ark and the flood came and destroyed them all.

"And the world will be as it was in the days of Lot: people went about their daily business—eating and drinking, buying and selling, farming and building—until the morning Lot left Sodom. Then fire and brimstone rained down from heaven and destroyed them all. Yes, it will be 'business as usual' right up to the hour of my return.

"Those away from home that day must not return to pack; those in the fields must not return to town—remember what happened to Lot's wife! Whoever clings to his life shall lose it, and whoever loses his life shall save it. That night two men will be asleep in the same room, and one will be taken away, the other left. Two women will be working together at household tasks; one will be taken, the other left; and so it will be with men working side by side in the fields."

"Lord, where will they be taken?" the disciples asked.

Jesus replied, "Where the body is, the vultures gather!"

18

One day Jesus told his disciples a story to illustrate their need for constant prayer and to show them that they must keep praying until the answer comes.

"There was a city judge," he said, "a very godless man who had great contempt for everyone. A widow of the city came to him frequently to appeal for justice against a man who had harmed her. The judge ignored her for a while, but eventually she got on his nerves.

" 'I fear neither God nor man,' he said to himself, 'but this woman bothers me. I'm going to see that she gets justice, for she is wearing me out with her constant coming!' "

Then the Lord said, "If even an evil judge can be worn down like that, don't you think that God will surely give justice to his people who plead with him day and night? Yes! He will answer them quickly! But the question is: When I, the Messiah, return, how many will I find who have faith [and are praying]?"

Then he told this story to some who boasted of their virtue and scorned everyone else:

"Two men went to the Temple to pray. One was a proud, self-righteous Pharisee, and the other a cheating tax collector. The proud Pharisee 'prayed' this prayer: 'Thank God, I am not a sinner like everyone else, especially like that tax collector over there! For I never cheat, I don't commit adultery, I go without food twice a week, and I give to God a tenth of everything I earn.'

"But the corrupt tax collector stood at a distance and dared not even lift his eyes to heaven as he prayed, but beat upon his chest in sorrow, exclaiming, 'God, be merciful to me, a sinner.' I tell you, this sinner, not the Pharisee, returned home forgiven! For the proud shall be humbled, but the humble shall be honored."

One day some mothers brought their babies to him to touch and bless. But the disciples told them to go away.

Then Jesus called the children over to him and said to the disciples, "Let the little children come to me! Never send them away! For the Kingdom of God belongs to men who have hearts as trusting as these little children's. And anyone who doesn't have their kind of faith will never get within the Kingdom's gates."

Once a Jewish religious leader asked him this question: "Good sir, what shall I do to get to heaven?"

"Do you realize what you are saying when you call me 'good'?" Jesus asked him. "Only God is truly good, and no one else.

"But as to your question, you know what the ten commandments say—don't commit adultery, don't murder, don't steal, don't lie, honor your parents, and so on." The man replied, "I've obeyed every one of these laws since I was a small child."

"There is still one thing you lack," Jesus said. "Sell all you have and give the money to the poor—it will become treasure for you in heaven—and come, follow me."

But when the man heard this he went sadly away, for he was very rich.

Jesus watched him go and then said to his disciples, "How hard it is for the rich to enter the Kingdom of God! It is easier for a camel to go through the eye of a needle than for a rich man to enter the Kingdom of God."

Those who heard him say this exclaimed, "If it is that hard, how can *anyone* be saved?"

He replied, "God can do what men can't!"

And Peter said, "We have left our homes and followed you."

"Yes," Jesus replied, "and everyone who has done as you have, leaving home, wife, brothers, parents, or children for the sake of the Kingdom of God, will be repaid many times over now, as well as receiving eternal life in the world to come."

Gathering the Twelve around him he told them, "As you know, we are going to Jerusalem. And when we get there, all the predictions of the ancient prophets concerning me will come true. I will be handed over to the Gentiles to be mocked and treated shamefully and spat upon, and lashed and killed. And the third day I will rise again."

But they didn't understand a thing he said. He seemed to be talking in riddles.

As they approached Jericho, a blind man was sitting beside the road, begging from travelers. When he heard the noise of a crowd going past, he asked what was happening. He was told that Jesus from Nazareth was going by, so he began shouting, "Jesus, Son of David, have mercy on me!"

The crowds ahead of Jesus tried to hush the man, but he only yelled the louder, "Son of David, have mercy on me!"

When Jesus arrived at the spot, he stopped. "Bring the blind man over here," he said. Then Jesus asked the man, "What do you want?"

"Lord," he pleaded, "I want to see!"

And Jesus said, "All right, begin seeing! Your faith has healed you."

And instantly the man could see, and followed Jesus, praising God. And all who saw it happen praised God too.

19

As Jesus was passing through Jericho, a man named Zacchaeus, one of the most influential Jews in the Roman tax-collecting business (and, of course, a very rich man), tried to get a look at Jesus, but he was too short to see over the crowds. So he ran ahead and climbed into a sycamore tree beside the road, to watch from there.

When Jesus came by he looked up at Zacchaeus and called him by name! "Zacchaeus!" he said. "Quick! Come down! For I am going to be a guest in your home today!"

Zacchaeus hurriedly climbed down and took Jesus to his house in great excitement and joy.

But the crowds were displeased. "He has gone to be the guest of a notorious sinner," they grumbled.

Meanwhile, Zacchaeus stood before the Lord and said, "Sir, from now on I will give half my wealth to the poor, and if I find I have overcharged anyone on his taxes, I will penalize myself by giving him back four times as much!"

Jesus told him, "This shows that salvation has come to this home today. This man was one of the lost sons of Abraham, and I, the Messiah, have come to search for and to save such souls as his."

And because Jesus was nearing Jerusalem, he told a story to correct the impression that the Kingdom of God would begin right away.

"A nobleman living in a certain province was called away to the distant capital of the empire to be crowned king of his province. Before he left he called together ten assistants and gave them each $2,000 to invest while he was gone. But some of his people hated him and sent him their declaration of independence, stating that they had rebelled and would not acknowledge him as their king.

"Upon his return he called in the men to whom he had given the money, to find out what they had done with it, and what their profits were.

"The first man reported a tremendous gain—ten times as much as the original amount!

" 'Fine!' the king exclaimed. 'You are a good man. You have been faithful with the little I entrusted to you, and as your reward, you shall be governor of ten cities.'

"The next man also reported a splendid gain—five times the original amount.

" 'All right!' his master said. 'You can be governor over five cities.'

"But the third man brought back only the money he had started with. 'I've kept it safe,' he said, 'because I was afraid [you would demand my profits], for you are a hard man to deal with, taking what isn't yours and even confiscating the crops that others plant.' 'You vile and wicked slave,' the king roared. 'Hard, am I? That's exactly how I'll be toward you! If you knew so much about me and how tough I am, then why didn't you deposit the money in the bank so that I could at least get some interest on it?'

"Then turning to the others standing by he ordered, 'Take the money away from him and give it to the man who earned the most.'

" 'But, sir,' they said, 'he has enough already!'

" 'Yes,' the king replied, 'but it is always true that those who have, get more, and those who have little, soon lose even that. And now about these enemies of mine who revolted—bring them in and execute them before me.' "

After telling this story, Jesus went on towards Jerusalem, walking along ahead of his disciples. As they came to the towns of Bethphage and Bethany, on the Mount of Olives, he sent two disciples ahead, with instructions to go to the next village, and as they entered they were to look for a donkey tied beside the road. It would be a colt, not yet broken for riding.

"Untie him," Jesus said, "and bring him here. And if anyone asks you what you are doing, just say, 'The Lord needs him.' "

They found the colt as Jesus said, and sure enough, as they were untying it, the owners demanded an explanation.

"What are you doing?" they asked. "Why are you untying our colt?"

And the disciples simply replied, "The Lord needs him!" So they brought the colt to Jesus and threw some of their clothing across its back for Jesus to sit on.

Then the crowds spread out their robes along the road ahead of him, and as they reached the place where the road started down from the Mount of Olives, the whole procession began to shout and sing as they walked along, praising God for all the wonderful miracles Jesus had done.

"God has given us a King!" they exulted. "Long live the King! Let all heaven rejoice! Glory to God in the highest heavens!"

But some of the Pharisees among the crowd said, "Sir, rebuke your followers for saying things like that!"

He replied, "If they keep quiet, the stones along the road will burst into cheers!"

But as they came closer to Jerusalem and he saw the city ahead, he began to cry. "Eternal peace was within your reach and you turned it down," he wept, "and now it is too late. Your enemies will pile up earth against your walls and encircle you and close in on you, and crush you to the ground, and your children within you; your enemies will not leave one stone upon another—for you have rejected the opportunity God offered you."

Then he entered the Temple and began to drive out the merchants from their stalls, saying to them, "The Scriptures declare, 'My Temple is a place of prayer; but you have turned it into a den of thieves.' "

After that he taught daily in the Temple, but the chief priests and other religious leaders and the business community were trying to find some way to get rid of him. But they could think of nothing, for he was a hero to the people—they hung on every word he said.

20

On one of those days when he was teaching and preaching the Good News in the Temple, he was confronted by the chief priests and other religious leaders and councilmen. They demanded to know by what authority he had driven out the merchants from the Temple.

"I'll ask you a question before I answer," he replied. "Was John sent by God, or was he merely acting under his own authority?"

They talked it over among themselves. "If we say his message was from heaven, then we are trapped because he will ask, 'Then why didn't you believe him?' But if we say John was not sent from God, the people will mob us, for they are convinced that he was a prophet." Finally they replied, "We don't know!"

And Jesus responded, "Then I won't answer your question either."

Now he turned to the people again and told them this story: "A man planted a vineyard and rented it out to some farmers, and went away to a distant land to live for several years. When harvest time came, he sent one of his men to the farm to collect his share of the crops. But the tenants beat him up and sent him back empty-handed. Then he sent another, but the same thing happened; he was beaten up and insulted and sent away without collecting. A third man was sent and the same thing happened. He, too, was wounded and chased away.

" 'What shall I do?' the owner asked himself. 'I know! I'll send my cherished son. Surely they will show respect for him.'

"But when the tenants saw his son, they said, 'This is our chance! This fellow will inherit all the land when his father dies. Come on. Let's kill him, and then it will be ours.' So they dragged him out of the vineyard and killed him.

"What do you think the owner will do? I'll tell you—he will come and kill them and rent the vineyard to others."

"But they would never do a thing like that," his listeners protested.

Jesus looked at them and said, "Then what does the Scripture mean where it says, 'The Stone rejected by the builders was made the cornerstone'?" And he added, "Whoever stumbles over that Stone shall be broken; and those on whom it falls will be crushed to dust."

When the chief priests and religious leaders heard about this story he had told, they wanted him arrested immediately, for they realized that he was talking about them. They were the wicked tenants in his illustration. But they were afraid that if they themselves arrested him there would bc a riot. So they tried to get him to say something that could be reported to the Roman governor as reason for arrest by him.

Watching their opportunity, they sent secret agents pretending to be honest men. They said to Jesus, "Sir, we know what an honest teacher you are. You always tell the truth and don't budge an inch in the face of what others think, but teach the ways of God. Now tell us—is it right to pay taxes to the Roman government or not?"

He saw through their trickery and said, "Show me a coin. Whose portrait is this on it? And whose name?"

They replied, "Caesar's—the Roman emperor's."

He said, "Then give the emperor all that is his—and give to God all that is his!"

Thus their attempt to outwit him before the people failed; and marveling at his answer, they were silent.

Then some Sadducees—men who believed that death is the end of existence, that there is no resurrection—came to Jesus with this:

"The laws of Moses state that if a man dies without children, the man's brother shall marry the widow and their children will legally belong to the dead man, to carry on his name. We know of a family of seven brothers. The oldest married and then died without any children. His brother married the widow and he, too, died. Still no children. And so it went, one after the other, until each of the seven had married her and died, leaving no children. Finally the woman died also. Now here is our question: Whose wife will she be in the resurrection? For all of them were married to her!"

Jesus replied, "Marriage is for people here on earth, but when those who are counted worthy of being raised from the dead get to heaven, they do not marry. And they never die again; in these respects they are like angels, and are sons of God, for they are raised up in new life from the dead.

"But as to your real question—whether or not there is a resurrection—why, even the writings of Moses himself prove this. For when he describes how God appeared to him in the burning bush, he speaks of God as 'the God of Abraham, the God of Isaac, and the God of Jacob.' To say that the Lord *is* some person's God means that person is *alive*, not dead! So from God's point of view, all men are living."

"Well said, sir!" remarked some of the experts in the Jewish law who were standing there. And that ended their questions, for they dared ask no more!

Then he presented *them* with a question. "Why is it," he asked, "that Christ, the Messiah, is said to be a descendant of King David? For David himself wrote in the book of Psalms: 'God said to my Lord, the Messiah, "Sit at my right hand until I place your enemies beneath your feet." ' How can the Messiah be both David's son and David's God at the same time?"

Then, with the crowds listening, he turned to his disciples and said, "Beware of these experts in religion, for they love to parade in dignified robes and to be bowed to by the people as they walk along the street. And how they love the seats of honor in the synagogues and at religious festivals! But even while they are praying long prayers with great outward piety, they are planning schemes to cheat widows out of their property. Therefore God's heaviest sentence awaits these men."

21

As he stood in the Temple, he was watching the rich tossing their gifts into the collection box. Then a poor widow came by and dropped in two small copper coins.

"Really," he remarked, "this poor widow has given more than all the rest of them combined. For they have given a little of what they didn't need, but she, poor as she is, has given everything she has."

Some of his disciples began talking about the beautiful stone-work of the Temple and the memorial decorations on the walls.

But Jesus said, "The time is coming when all these things you are admiring will be knocked down, and not one stone will be left on top of another; all will become one vast heap of rubble."

"Master!" they exclaimed. "When? And will there be any warning ahead of time?"

He replied, "Don't let anyone mislead you. For many will come announcing themselves as the Messiah, and saying, 'The time has come.' But don't believe them! And when you hear of wars and insurrections beginning, don't panic. True, wars must come, but the end won't follow immediately—for nation shall rise against nation and kingdom against kingdom, and there will be great earthquakes, and famines in many lands, and epidemics, and terrifying things happening in the heavens.

"But before all this occurs, there will be a time of special persecution, and you will be dragged into synagogues and prisons and before kings and governors for my name's sake. But as a result, the Messiah will be widely known and honored. Therefore, don't be concerned about how to answer the charges against you, for I will give you the right words and such logic that none of your opponents will be able to reply! Even those closest to you—your parents, brothers, relatives, and friends will betray you and have you arrested; and some of you will be killed. And everyone will hate you because you are mine and are called by my name. But not a hair of your head will perish! For if you stand firm, you will win your souls.

"But when you see Jerusalem surrounded by armies, then you will know that the time of its destruction has arrived. Then let the people of Judea flee to the hills. Let those in Jerusalem try to escape, and those outside the city must not attempt to return. For those will be days of God's judgment, and the words of the ancient Scriptures written by the prophets will be abundantly fulfilled. Woe to expectant mothers in those days, and those with tiny babies. For there will be great distress upon this nation and wrath upon this people. They will be brutally killed by enemy weapons, or sent away as exiles and captives to all the nations of thc world; and Jerusalem shall be conquered and trampled down by the Gentiles until the period of Gentile triumph ends in God's good time.

"Then there will be strange events in the skies—warnings, evil omens and portents in the sun, moon and stars; and down here on earth the nations will be in turmoil, perplexed by the roaring seas and strange tides. The courage of many people will falter because of the fearful fate they see coming upon the earth, for the stability of the very heavens will be broken up. Then the peoples of the earth shall see me, the Messiah, coming in a cloud with power and great glory. So when all these things begin to happen, stand straight and look up! For your salvation is near."

Then he gave them this illustration: "Notice the fig tree, or any other tree. When the leaves come out, you know without being told that summer is near. In the same way, when you see the events taking place that I've described you can be just as sure that the Kingdom of God is near.

"I solemnly declare to you that when these things happen, the end of this age has come. And though all heaven and earth shall pass away, yet my words remain forever true.

"Watch out! Don't let my sudden coming catch you unawares; don't let me find you living in careless ease, carousing and drinking, and occupied with the problems of this life, like all the rest of the world. Keep a constant watch. And pray that if possible you may arrive in my presence without having to experience these horrors."

Every day Jesus went to the Temple to teach, and the crowds began gathering early in the morning to hear him. And each evening he returned to spend the night on the Mount of Olives.

22

And now the Passover celebration was drawing near—the Jewish festival when only bread made without yeast was used. The chief priests and other religious leaders were actively plotting Jesus' murder, trying to find a way to kill him without starting a riot—a possibility they greatly feared.

Then Satan entered into Judas Iscariot, who was one of the twelve disciples, and he went over to the chief priests and captains of the Temple guards to discuss the best way to betray Jesus to them. They were, of course, delighted to know that he was ready to help them and promised him a reward. So he began to look for an opportunity for them to arrest Jesus quietly when the crowds weren't around.

Now the day of the Passover celebration arrived, when the Passover lamb was killed and eaten with the unleavened bread. Jesus sent Peter and John ahead to find a place to prepare their Passover meal.

"Where do you want us to go?" they asked.

And he replied, "As soon as you enter Jerusalem, you will see a man walking along carrying a pitcher of water. Follow him into the house he enters, and say to the man who lives there, 'Our Teacher says for you to show us the guest room where he can eat the Passover meal with his disciples.' He will take you upstairs to a large room all ready for us. That is the place. Go ahead and prepare the meal there."

They went off to the city and found everything just as Jesus had said, and prepared the Passover supper.

Then Jesus and the others arrived, and at the proper time all sat down together at the table; and he said, "I have looked forward to this hour with deep longing, anxious to eat this Passover meal with you before my suffering begins. For I tell you now that I won't eat it again until what it represents has occurred in the Kingdom of God."

Then he took a glass of wine, and when he had given thanks for it, he said, "Take this and share it among yourselves. For I will not drink wine again until the Kingdom of God has come."

Then he took a loaf of bread; and when he had thanked God for it, he broke it apart and gave it to them, saying, "This is my body, given for you. Eat it in remembrance of me."

After supper he gave them another glass of wine, saying, "This wine is the token of God's new agreement to save you—an agreement sealed with the blood I shall pour out to purchase back your souls. But here at this table, sitting among us as a friend, is the man who will betray me. I must die. It is part of God's plan. But, oh, the horror awaiting that man who betrays me."

Then the disciples wondered among themselves which of them would ever do such a thing.

And they began to argue among themselves as to who would have the highest rank [in the coming Kingdom].

Jesus told them, "In this world the kings and great men order their slaves around, and the slaves have no choice but to like it! But among you, the one who serves you best will be your leader. Out in the world the master sits at the table and is served by his servants. But not here! For I am your servant. Nevertheless, because you have stood true to me in these terrible days, and because my Father has granted me a Kingdom, I, here and now, grant you the right to eat and drink at my table in that Kingdom; and you will sit on thrones judging the twelve tribes of Israel.

"Simon, Simon, Satan has asked to have you, to sift you like wheat, but I have pleaded in prayer for you that your faith should not completely fail. So when you have repented and turned to me again, strengthen and build up the faith of your brothers."

Simon said, "Lord, I am ready to go to jail with you, and even to die with you."

But Jesus said, "Peter, let me tell you something. Between now and tomorrow morning when the rooster crows, you will deny me three times, declaring that you don't even know me."

Then Jesus asked them, "When I sent you out to preach the Good News and you were without money, duffle bag, or extra clothing, how did you get along?"

"Fine," they replied.

"But now," he said, "take a duffle bag if you have one, and your money. And if you don't have a sword, better sell your clothes and buy one! For the time has come for this prophecy about me to come true: 'He will be condemned as a criminal!' Yes, everything written about me by the prophets will come true."

"Master," they replied, "we have two swords among us."

"Enough!" he said.

Then, accompanied by the disciples, he left the upstairs room and went as usual to the Mount of Olives. There he told them, "Pray God that you will not be overcome by temptation."

He walked away, perhaps a stone's throw, and knelt down and prayed this prayer: "Father, if you are willing, please take away this cup of horror from me. But I want your will, not mine." Then an angel from heaven appeared and strengthened him, for he was in such agony of spirit that he broke into a sweat of blood, with great drops falling to the ground as he prayed more and more earnestly. At last he stood up again and returned to the disciples—only to find them asleep, exhausted from grief.

"Asleep!" he said. "Get up! Pray God that you will not fall when you are tempted."

But even as he said this, a mob approached, led by Judas, one of his twelve disciples. Judas walked over to Jesus and kissed him on the cheek in friendly greeting.

But Jesus said, "Judas, how can you do this—betray the Messiah with a kiss?"

When the other disciples saw what was about to happen, they

exclaimed, "Master, shall we fight? We brought along the swords!" And one of them slashed at the High Priest's servant, and cut off his right ear.

But Jesus said, "Don't resist any more." And he touched the place where the man's ear had been and restored it. Then Jesus addressed the chief priests and captains of the Temple guards and the religious leaders who headed the mob. "Am I a robber," he asked, "that you have come armed with swords and clubs to get me? Why didn't you arrest me in the Temple? I was there every day. But this is your moment—the time when Satan's power reigns supreme."

So they seized him and led him to the High Priest's residence, and Peter followed at a distance. The soldiers lit a fire in the courtyard and sat around it for warmth, and Peter joined them there.

A servant girl noticed him in the firelight and began staring at him. Finally she spoke: "This man was with Jesus!"

Peter denied it. "Woman," he said, "I don't even know the man!"

After a while someone else looked at him and said, "You must be one of them!"

"No sir, I am not!" Peter replied.

About an hour later someone else flatly stated, "I know this fellow is one of Jesus' disciples, for both are from Galilee."

But Peter said, "Man, I don't know what you are talking about." And as he said the words, a rooster crowed.

At that moment Jesus turned and looked at Peter. Then Peter remembered what he had said—"Before the rooster crows tomorrow morning, you will deny me three times." And Peter walked out of the courtyard, crying bitterly.

Now the guards in charge of Jesus began mocking him. They blindfolded him and hit him with their fists and asked, "Who hit you that time, prophet?" And they threw all sorts of other insults at him.

Early the next morning at daybreak the Jewish Supreme Court assembled, including the chief priests and all the top religious authorities of the nation. Jesus was led before this Council, and instructed to state whether or not he claimed to be the Messiah.

But he replied, "If I tell you, you won't believe me or let me present my case. But the time is soon coming when I, the Messiah, shall be enthroned beside Almighty God."

They all shouted, "Then you claim you are the Son of God?"

And he replied, "Yes, I am."

"What need do we have for other witnesses?" they shouted. "For we ourselves have heard him say it."

23

Then the entire Council took Jesus over to Pilate, the governor. They began at once accusing him: "This fellow has been leading our people to ruin by telling them not to pay their taxes to the Roman government and by claiming he is our Messiah—a King."

So Pilate asked him, "Are you their Messiah—their King?"

"Yes," Jesus replied, "it is as you say."

Then Pilate turned to the chief priests and to the mob and said, "So? That isn't a crime!"

Then they became desperate. "But he is causing riots against the government everywhere he goes, all over Judea, from Galilee to Jerusalem!"

"Is he then a Galilean?" Pilate asked.

When they told him yes, Pilate said to take him to King Herod, for Galilee was under Herod's jurisdiction; and Herod happened to be in Jerusalem at the time. Herod was delighted at the opportunity to see Jesus, for he had heard a lot about him and had been hoping to see him perform a miracle.

He asked Jesus question after question, but there was no reply. Meanwhile, the chief priests and the other religious leaders stood there shouting their accusations.

Now Herod and his soldiers began mocking and ridiculing

Jesus; and putting a kingly robe on him, they sent him back to Pilate. That day Herod and Pilate—enemies before—became fast friends.

Then Pilate called together the chief priests and other Jewish leaders, along with the people, and announced his verdict:

"You brought this man to me, accusing him of leading a revolt against the Roman government. I have examined him thoroughly on this point and find him innocent. Herod came to the same conclusion and sent him back to us—nothing this man has done calls for the death penalty. I will therefore have him scourged with leaded thongs, and release him."

But now a mighty roar rose from the crowd as with one voice they shouted, "Kill him, and release Barabbas to us!" (Barabbas was in prison for starting an insurrection in Jerusalem against the government, and for murder.) Pilate argued with them, for he wanted to release Jesus. But they shouted, "Crucify him! Crucify him!"

Once more, for the third time, he demanded, "Why? What crime has he committed? I have found no reason to sentence him to death. I will therefore scourge him and let him go." But they shouted louder and louder for Jesus' death, and their voices prevailed.

So Pilate sentenced Jesus to die as they demanded. And he released Barabbas, the man in prison for insurrection and murder, at their request. But he delivered Jesus over to them to do with as they would.

As the crowd led Jesus away to his death, Simon of Cyrene, who was just coming into Jerusalem from the country, was forced to follow, carrying Jesus' cross. Great crowds trailed along behind, and many grief-stricken women.

But Jesus turned and said to them, "Daughters of Jerusalem, don't weep for me, but for yourselves and for your children. For the days are coming when the women who have no children will be counted fortunate indeed. Mankind will beg the mountains to fall on them and crush them, and the hills to bury them. For if such things as this are done to me, the Living Tree, what will they do to you?"

Two others, criminals, were led out to be executed with him at a place called "The Skull." There all three were crucified—Jesus on the center cross, and the two criminals on either side.

"Father, forgive these people," Jesus said, "for they don't know what they are doing."

And the soldiers gambled for his clothing, throwing dice for each piece. The crowd watched. And the Jewish leaders laughed and scoffed. "He was so good at helping others," they said, "let's see him save himself if he is really God's Chosen One, the Messiah."

The soldiers mocked him, too, by offering him a drink—of sour wine. And they called to him, "If you are the King of the Jews, save yourself!"

A signboard was nailed to the cross above him with these words: "This is the king of the Jews."

One of the criminals hanging beside him scoffed, "So you're the Messiah, are you? Prove it by saving yourself—and us, too, while you're at it!"

But the other criminal protested. "Don't you even fear God when you are dying? We deserve to die for our evil deeds, but this man hasn't done one thing wrong." Then he said, "Jesus, remember me when you come into your Kingdom."

And Jesus replied, "Today you will be with me in Paradise. This is a solemn promise."

By now it was noon, and darkness fell across the whole land for three hours, until three o'clock. The light from the sun was gone—and suddenly the thick veil hanging in the Temple split apart.

Then Jesus shouted, "Father, I commit my spirit to you," and with those words he died.

When the captain of the Roman military unit handling the executions saw what had happened, he was stricken with awe before God and said, "Surely this man was innocent."

And when the crowd that came to see the crucifixion saw that Jesus was dead, they went home in deep sorrow. Meanwhile, Jesus' friends, including the women who had followed him down from Galilee, stood in the distance watching.

Then a man named Joseph, a member of the Jewish Supreme Court, from the city of Arimathea in Judea, went to Pilate and asked for the body of Jesus. He was a godly man who had been expecting the Messiah's coming and had not agreed with the decision and actions of the other Jewish leaders. So he took down Jesus' body and wrapped it in a long linen cloth and laid it in a new, unused tomb hewn into the rock [at the side of a hill]. This was done late on Friday afternoon, the day of preparation for the Sabbath.

As the body was taken away, the women from Galilee followed and saw it carried into the tomb. Then they went home and prepared spices and ointments to embalm him; but by the time they were finished it was the Sabbath, so they rested all that day as required by the Jewish law.

24

But very early on Sunday morning they took the ointments to the tomb—and found that the huge stone covering the entrance had been rolled aside. So they went in—but the Lord Jesus' body was gone.

They stood there puzzled, trying to think what could have happened to it. Suddenly two men appeared before them, clothed in shining robes so bright their eyes were dazzled. The women were terrified and bowed low before them.

Then the men asked, "Why are you looking in a tomb for someone who is alive? He isn't here! He has come back to life again! Don't you remember what he told you back in Galilee—that the Messiah must be betrayed into the power of evil men and be crucified and that he would rise again the third day?"

Then they remembered, and rushed back to Jerusalem to tell his eleven disciples—and everyone else—what had happened. (The women who went to the tomb were Mary Magdalene and Joanna and Mary the mother of James, and several others.) But the story sounded like a fairy tale to the men—they didn't believe it.

However, Peter ran to the tomb to look. Stooping, he peered in and saw the empty linen wrappings; and then he went back home again, wondering what had happened.

That same day, Sunday, two of Jesus' followers were walking to the village of Emmaus, seven miles out of Jerusalem. As they walked along they were talking of Jesus' death, when suddenly Jesus himself came along and joined them and began walking beside them. But they didn't recognize him, for God kept them from it.

"You seem to be in a deep discussion about something," he said. "What are you so concerned about?" They stopped short, sadness written across their faces. And one of them, Cleopas, replied, "You must be the only person in Jerusalem who hasn't heard about the terrible things that happened there last week."

"What things?" Jesus asked.

"The things that happened to Jesus, the Man from Nazareth," they said. "He was a Prophet who did incredible miracles and was a mighty Teacher, highly regarded by both God and man. But the chief priests and our religious leaders arrested him and handed him over to the Roman government to be condemned to death, and they crucified him. We had thought he was the glorious Messiah and that he had come to rescue Israel.

"And now, besides all this—which happened three days ago—some women from our group of his followers were at his tomb early this morning and came back with an amazing report that his body was missing, and that they had seen some angels there who told them Jesus is alive! Some of our men ran out to see, and sure enough, Jesus' body was gone, just as the women had said."

Then Jesus said to them, "You are such foolish, foolish people! You find it so hard to believe all that the prophets wrote in the Scriptures! Wasn't it clearly predicted by the prophets that the Messiah would have to suffer all these things before entering his time of glory?"

Then Jesus quoted them passage after passage from the writings of the prophets, beginning with the book of Genesis and going right on through the Scriptures, explaining what the passages meant and what they said about himself.

By this time they were nearing Emmaus and the end of their journey. Jesus would have gone on, but they begged him to stay the night with them, as it was getting late. So he went home with them. As they sat down to eat, he asked God's blessing on the food and then took a small loaf of bread and broke it and was passing it over to them, when suddenly—it was as though their eyes were opened—they recognized him! And at that moment he disappeared!

They began telling each other how their hearts had felt strangely warm as he talked with them and explained the Sciptures during the walk down the road. Within the hour they were on their way back to Jerusalem, where the eleven disciples and the other followers of Jesus greeted them with these words, "The Lord has really risen! He appeared to Peter!"

Then the two from Emmaus told their story of how Jesus had appeared to them as they were walking along the road and how they had recognized him as he was breaking the bread.

And just as they were telling about it, Jesus himself was suddenly standing there among them, and greeted them. But the whole group was terribly frightened, thinking they were seeing a ghost!

"Why are you frightened?" he asked. "Why do you doubt that it is really I? Look at my hands! Look at my feet! You can see that it is I, myself! Touch me and make sure that I am not a ghost! For ghosts don't have bodies, as you see that I do!" As he spoke, he held out his hands for them to see [the marks of the nails], and showed them [the wounds in] his feet.

Still they stood there undecided, filled with joy and doubt.

Then he asked them, "Do you have anything here to eat?"

They gave him a piece of broiled fish, and he ate it as they watched!

Then he said, "When I was with you before, don't you remember my telling you that everything written about me by Moses and the prophets and in the Psalms must all come true?" Then he opened their minds to understand at last these many Scriptures! And he said, "Yes, it was written long ago that the Messiah must suffer and die and rise again from the dead on the third day; and that this message of salvation should be taken from Jerusalem to all the nations: *There is forgiveness of sins for all who turn to me*. You have seen these prophecies come true.

"And now I will send the Holy Spirit upon you, just as my Father promised. Don't begin telling others yet—stay here in the city until the Holy Spirit comes and fills you with power from heaven."

Then Jesus led them out along the road to Bethany, and lifting his hands to heaven, he blessed them, and then began rising into the sky, and went on to heaven. And they worshiped him, and returned to Jerusalem filled with mighty joy, and were continually in the Temple, praising God.

Part 2

The True Story of Jesus' Earliest Followers

1

Dear friend who loves God:

In my first letter I told you about Jesus' life and teachings and how he returned to heaven after giving his chosen apostles further instructions from the Holy Spirit. During the forty days after his crucifixion he appeared to the apostles from time to time, actually alive, and proved to them in many ways that it was really he himself they were seeing. And on these occasions he talked to them about the Kingdom of God.

In one of these meetings he told them not to leave Jerusalem until the Holy Spirit came upon them in fulfillment of the Father's promise, a matter he had previously discussed with them.

"John baptized you with water," he reminded them, "but you shall be baptized with the Holy Spirit in just a few days."

And another time when he appeared to them, they asked him, "Lord, are you going to free Israel [from Rome] now and restore us as an independent nation?"

"The Father sets those dates," he replied, "and they are not for you to know. But when the Holy Spirit has come upon you, you will receive power to testify about me with great effect, to the people in Jerusalem, throughout Judea, in Samaria, and to the ends of the earth, about my death and resurrection."

It was not long afterwards that he rose into the sky and disappeared into a cloud, leaving them staring after him. As they were straining their eyes for another glimpse, suddenly two white-robed men were standing there among them, and said, "Men of Galilee, why are you standing here staring at the sky? Jesus has gone away to heaven, and some day, just as he went, he will return!"

They were at the Mount of Olives when this happened, so now they walked the half mile back to Jerusalem and held a prayer meeting in an upstairs room of the house where they were staying.

Here is the list of those who were present at the meeting: Peter, John, James, Andrew, Philip, Thomas, Bartholomew, Matthew, James (son of Alphaeus), Simon (also called "The Zealot"), Judas (son of James), and the brothers of Jesus. Several women, including Jesus' mother, were also there.

This prayer meeting went on for several days. During this time, on a day when about 120 people were present, Peter stood up and addressed them as follows:

"Brothers, it was necessary for the Scriptures to come true concerning Judas, who betrayed Jesus by guiding the mob to him, for this was predicted long ago by the Holy Spirit, speaking through King David. Judas was one of us, chosen to be an apostle just as we were. He bought a field with the money he received for his treachery and falling headlong there, he burst open, spilling out his bowels. The news of his death spread rapidly among all the people of Jerusalem, and they named the place 'The Field of Blood.' King David's prediction of this appears in the Book of Psalms, where he says, 'Let his home become desolate with no one living in it.' And again, 'Let his work be given to someone else to do.'

"So now we must choose someone else to take Judas' place and to join us as witnesses of Jesus' resurrection. Let us select someone who has been with us constantly from our first association with the Lord—from the time he was baptized by John until the day he was taken from us into heaven."

The assembly nominated two men: Joseph Justus (also called Barsabbas) and Matthias. Then they all prayed for the right man to be chosen. "O Lord," they said, "you know every heart; show us which of these men you have chosen as an apostle to replace Judas the traitor, who has gone on to his proper place."

Then they drew straws, and in this manner Matthias was chosen and became an apostle with the other eleven.

2

Seven weeks had gone by since Jesus' death and resurrection, and the Day of Pentecost had now arrived. As the believers met together that day, suddenly there was a sound like the roaring of a mighty windstorm in the skies above them and it filled the house where they were meeting. Then, what looked like flames or tongues of fire appeared and settled on their heads. And everyone present was filled with the Holy Spirit and began speaking in other tongues, for the Holy Spirit gave them this ability.

Many godly Jews were in Jerusalem that day for the religious celebrations, having arrived from many nations. And when they heard the roaring in the sky above the house, crowds came running to see what it was all about, and were stunned to hear their own languages being spoken by the disciples.

"How can this be?" they exclaimed. "For these men are all from Galilee, and yet we hear them speaking all the native languages of the lands where we were born! Here we are—Parthians, Medes, Elamites, men from Mesopotamia, Judea, Cappadocia, Pontus, Ausia, Phrygia, Pamphylia, Egypt, the Cyrene language areas of Libya, visitors from Rome—both Jews and Jewish converts—Cretans, and Arabians. And we all hear these men telling in our own languages about the mighty miracles of God!"

They stood there amazed and perplexed. "What can this mean?" they asked each other.

But others in the crowd were mocking. "They're drunk, that's all!" they said.

Then Peter stepped forward with the eleven apostles, and shouted to the crowd, "Listen, all of you, visitors and residents of Jerusalem alike! Some of you are saying these men are drunk! It isn't true! It's much too early for that! People don't get drunk by 9 A.M.! No! What you see this morning was predicted centuries ago by the prophet Joel—'In the last days,' God said, 'I will pour out my Holy Spirit upon all mankind, and your sons and daughters shall prophesy, and your young men shall see visions, and your old men dream dreams. Yes, the Holy Spirit shall come upon all my servants, men and women alike, and they shall prophesy. And I will cause strange demonstrations in the heavens and on the earth—blood and fire and clouds of smoke; the sun shall turn black and the moon blood-red before that awesome Day of the Lord arrives. But anyone who asks for mercy from the Lord shall have it and shall be saved.'

"O men of Israel, listen! God publicly endorsed Jesus of Nazareth by doing tremendous miracles through him, as you well know. But God, following his prearranged plan, let you use the Roman government to nail him to the cross and murder him. Then God released him from the horrors of death and brought him back to life again, for death could not keep this man within its grip.

"King David quoted Jesus as saying:

'I know the Lord is always with me. He is helping me. God's mighty power supports me.

No wonder my heart is filled with joy and my tongue shouts his praises! For I know all will be well with me in death—

You will not leave my soul in hell or let the body of your Holy Son decay.

You will give me back my life, and give me wonderful joy in your presence.'

"Dear brothers, think! David wasn't referring to himself when he spoke these words I have quoted, for he died and was buried, and his tomb is still here among us. But he was a prophet, and knew God had promised with an unbreakable oath that one of David's own descendants would [be the Messiah and] sit on David's throne.

David was looking far into the future and predicting the Messiah's resurrection, and saying that the Messiah's soul would not be left in hell and his body would not decay. He was speaking of Jesus, and we all are witnesses that Jesus rose from the dead.

"And now he sits on the throne of highest honor in heaven, next to God. And just as promised, the Father gave him the authority to send the Holy Spirit—with the results you are seeing and hearing today.

"[No, David was not speaking of himself in these words of his I have quoted], for he never ascended into the skies. Moreover, he further stated, 'God spoke to my Lord, the Messiah, and said to him, Sit here in honor beside me until I bring your enemies into complete subjection.'

"Therefore I clearly state to everyone in Israel that God has made this Jesus you crucified to be the Lord, the Messiah!"

These words of Peter's moved them deeply, and they said to him and to the other apostles, "Brothers, what should we do?"

And Peter replied, "Each one of you must turn from sin, return to God, and be baptized in the name of Jesus Christ for the forgiveness of your sins; then you also shall receive this gift, the Holy Spirit. For Christ promised him to each one of you who has been called by the Lord our God, and to your children and even to those in distant lands!"

Then Peter preached a long sermon, telling about Jesus and strongly urging all his listeners to save themselves from the evils of their nation. And those who believed Peter were baptized—about 3,000 in all! They joined with the other believers in regular attendance at the apostles' teaching sessions and at the Communion services and prayer meetings. A deep sense of awe was on them all, and the apostles did many miracles.

And all the believers met together constantly and shared everything with each other, selling their possessions and dividing with those in need. They worshiped together regularly at the Temple each day, met in small groups in homes for Communion, and shared their meals with great joy and thankfulness, praising God. The whole city was favorable to them, and each day God added to them all who were being saved.

3

Peter and John went to the Temple one afternoon to take part in the three o'clock daily prayer meeting. As they approached the Temple, they saw a man lame from birth carried along the street and laid beside the Temple gate—the one called The Beautiful Gate—as was his custom every day. As Peter and John were passing by, he asked them for some money.

They looked at him intently, and then Peter said, "Look here!"

The lame man looked at them eagerly, expecting a gift.

But Peter said, "We don't have any money for you! But I'll give you something else! I command you in the name of Jesus Christ of Nazareth, *walk!*"

Then Peter took the lame man by the hand and pulled him to his feet. And as he did, the man's feet and ankle-bones were healed and strengthened so that he came up with a leap, stood there a moment and began walking! Then, walking, leaping, and praising God, he went into the Temple with them.

When the people inside saw him walking and heard him praising God, and realized he was the lame beggar they had seen so often at The Beautiful Gate, they were inexpressibly surprised! They all rushed out to Solomon's Hall, where he was holding tightly to Peter and John! Everyone stood there awed by the wonderful thing that had happened.

Peter saw his opportunity and addressed the crowd. "Men of Israel," he said, "what is so surprising about this? And why look at us as though we by our own power and godliness had made this man walk? For it is the God of Abraham, Isaac, Jacob and of all our ancestors who has brought glory to his servant Jesus by doing this. I refer to the Jesus whom you rejected before Pilate, despite Pilate's determination to release him. You didn't want him freed—this holy, righteous one. Instead you demanded the release of a murderer. And you killed the Author of Life; but God brought him back to life again. And John and I are witnesses of this fact, for after you killed him we saw him alive!

"Jesus' name has healed this man—and you know how lame he was before. Faith in Jesus' name—faith given us from God—has caused this perfect healing.

"Dear brothers, I realize that what you did to Jesus was done in ignorance; and the same can be said of your leaders. But God was fulfilling the prophecies that the Messiah must suffer all these things. Now change your mind and attitude to God and turn to him so he can cleanse away your sins and send you wonderful times of refreshment from the presence of the Lord and send Jesus your Messiah back to you again. For he must remain in heaven until the final recovery of all things from sin, as prophesied from ancient times. Moses, for instance, said long ago, 'The Lord God will raise up a Prophet among you, who will resemble me! Listen carefully to everything he tells you. Anyone who will not listen to him shall be utterly destroyed.'

"Samuel and every prophet since have all spoken about what is going on today. You are the children of those prophets; and you are included in God's promise to your ancestors to bless the entire world through the Jewish race—that is the promise God gave to Abraham. And as soon as God had brought his servant to life again, he sent him first of all to you men of Israel, to bless you by turning you back from your sins."

4

While they were talking to the people, the chief priests, the captain of the Temple police, and some of the Sadducees came over to them, very disturbed that Peter and John were claiming that Jesus had risen from the dead. They arrested them and since it was already evening, jailed them overnight. But many of the people who heard their message believed it, so that the number of believers now reached a new high of about 5,000 men!

The next day it happened that the Council of all the Jewish leaders was in session in Jerusalem—Annas the High Priest was there, and Caiaphas, John, Alexander, and others of the High Priest's relatives. So the two disciples were brought in before them.

"By what power, or by whose authority have you done this?" the Council demanded.

Then Peter, filled with the Holy Spirit, said to them, "Honorable leaders and elders of our nation, if you mean the good deed done to the cripple, and how he was healed, let me clearly state to you and to all the people of Israel that it was done in the name and power of Jesus from Nazareth, the Messiah, the man you crucified—but God raised back to life again. It is by his authority that this man stands here healed! For Jesus the Messiah is (the one referred to in the Scriptures when they speak of) a 'stone discarded by the builders which became the capstone of the arch.' There is salvation in no one else! Under all heaven there is no other name for men to call upon to save them."

When the Council saw the boldness of Peter and John, and could see that they were obviously uneducated non-professionals, they were amazed and realized what being with Jesus had done for them! And the Council could hardly discredit the healing when the man they had healed was standing right there beside them! So they sent them out of the Council chamber and conferred among themselves.

"What shall we do with these men?" they asked each other. "We can't deny that they have done a tremendous miracle, and everybody in Jerusalem knows about it. But perhaps we can stop them from spreading their propaganda. We'll tell them that if they do it again we'll really throw the book at them." So they called them back in, and told them never again to speak about Jesus.

But Peter and John replied, "You decide whether God wants us to obey you instead of him! We cannot stop telling about the wonderful things we saw Jesus do and heard him say."

The Council then threatened them further, and finally let them go because they didn't know how to punish them without starting a riot. For everyone was praising God for this wonderful miracle—the healing of a man who had been lame for forty years.

As soon as they were freed, Peter and John found the other disciples and told them what the Council had said.

Then all the believers united in this prayer:

"O Lord, Creator of heaven and earth and of the sea and everything in them—you spoke long ago by the Holy Spirit through our ancestor King David, your servant, saying, 'Why do the heathen rage against the Lord, and the foolish nations plan their little plots against Almighty God? The kings of the earth unite to fight against him, and against the anointed Son of God!'

"That is what is happening here in this city today! For Herod the king, and Pontius Pilate the governor, and all the Romans—as well as the people of Israel—are united against Jesus, your anointed Son, your holy servant. They won't stop at anything that you in your wise power will let them do. And now, O Lord, hear their threats, and grant to your servants great boldness in their preaching, and send your healing power, and may miracles and wonders be done by the name of your holy servant Jesus."

After this prayer, the building where they were meeting shook and they were all filled with the Holy Spirit and boldly preached God's message.

All the believers were of one heart and mind, and no one felt that what he owned was his own; everyone was sharing. And the apostles preached powerful sermons about the resurrection of the Lord Jesus, and there was warm fellowship among all the believers, and no poverty—for all who owned land or houses sold them and brought the money to the apostles to give to others in need.

For instance, there was Joseph (the one the apostles nicknamed "Barny the Preacher"! He was of the tribe of Levi, from the island of Cyprus). He was one of those who sold a field he owned and brought the money to the apostles for distribution to those in need.

5

But there was a man named Ananias (with his wife Sapphira) who sold some property, and brought only part of the money, claiming it was the full price. (His wife had agreed to this deception.)

But Peter said, "Ananias, Satan has filled your heart. When you claimed this was the full price, you were lying to the Holy Spirit. The property was yours to sell or not, as you wished. And after selling it, it was yours to decide how much to give. How could you do a thing like this? You weren't lying to us, but to God."

As soon as Ananias heard these words, he fell to the floor, dead! Everyone was terrified, and the younger men covered him with a sheet and took him out and buried him.

About three hours later his wife came in, not knowing what had happened. Peter asked her, "Did you people sell your land for such and such a price?"

"Yes," she replied, "we did."

And Peter said, "How could you and your husband even think of doing a thing like this—conspiring together to test the Spirit of God's ability to know what is going on? Just outside that door are the young men who buried your husband, and they will carry you out too."

Instantly she fell to the floor, dead, and the young men came in and, seeing that she was dead, carried her out and buried her beside her husband. Terror gripped the entire church and all others who heard what had happened.

Meanwhile, the apostles were meeting regularly at the Temple in the area known as Solomon's Hall, and they did many remarkable miracles among the people. The other believers didn't dare join them, though, but all had the highest regard for them. And more and more believers were added to the Lord, crowds both of men and women. Sick people were brought out into the streets on beds and mats so that at least Peter's shadow would fall across some of them as he went by! And crowds came in from the Jerusalem suburbs, bringing their sick folk and those possessed by demons; and every one of them was healed.

The High Priest and his relatives and friends among the Sadducees reacted with violent jealousy and arrested the apostles, and put them in the public jail.

But an angel of the Lord came at night, opened the gates of the jail and brought them out. Then he told them, "Go over to the Temple and preach about this Life!"

They arrived at the Temple about daybreak, and immediately began preaching! Later that morning the High Priest and his courtiers arrived at the Temple, and, convening the Jewish Council and the entire Senate, they sent for the apostles to be brought for trial. But when the police arrived at the jail, the men weren't there, so they returned to the Council and reported, "The jail doors were locked, and the guards were standing outside, but when we opened the gates, no one was there!"

When the police captain and the chief priests heard this, they were frantic, wondering what would happen next and where all this would end! Then someone arrived with the news that the men they had jailed were out in the Temple, preaching to the people!

The police captain went with his officers and arrested them (without violence, for they were afraid the people would kill them if they roughed up the disciples) and brought them in before the Council.

"Didn't we tell you never again to preach about this Jesus?" the High Priest demanded. "And instead you have filled all Jerusalem with your teaching and intend to bring the blame for this man's death on us!"

But Peter and the apostles replied, "We must obey God rather than men. The God of our ancestors brought Jesus back to life again after you had killed him by hanging him on a cross. Then, with mighty power, God exalted him to be a Prince and Savior, so that the people of Israel would have an opportunity for repentance, and for their sins to be forgiven. And we are witnesses of these things, and so is the Holy Spirit, who is given by God to all who obey him."

At this, the Council was furious, and decided to kill them. But one of their members, a Pharisee named Gamaliel (an expert on religious law and very popular with the people), stood up and requested that the apostles be sent outside the Council chamber while he talked.

Then he addressed his colleagues as follows:

"Men of Israel, take care what you are planning to do to these men! Some time ago there was that fellow Theudas, who pretended to be someone great. About 400 others joined him, but he was killed, and his followers were harmlessly dispersed.

"After him, at the time of the taxation, there was Judas of Galilee. He drew away some people as disciples, but he also died, and his followers scattered.

"And so my advice is, leave these men alone. If what they teach and do is merely on their own, it will soon be overthrown. But if it is of God, you will not be able to stop them, lest you find yourselves fighting even against God."

The Council accepted his advice, called in the apostles, had them beaten, and then told them never again to speak in the name of Jesus, and finally let them go. They left the Council chamber rejoicing that God had counted them worthy to suffer dishonor for his name. And every day, in the Temple and in their home Bible classes, they continued to teach and preach that Jesus is the Messiah.

6

But with the believers multiplying rapidly, there were rumblings of discontent. Those who spoke only Greek complained that their widows were being discriminated against, that they were not being given as much food, in the daily distribution, as the widows who spoke Hebrew. So the Twelve called a meeting of all the believers.

"We should spend our time preaching, not administering a feeding program," they said. "Now look around among yourselves, dear brothers, and select seven men, wise and full of the Holy Spirit, who are well thought of by everyone; and we will put them in charge of this business. Then we can spend our time in prayer, preaching, and teaching."

This sounded reasonable to the whole assembly, and they elected the following: Stephen (a man unusually full of faith and the Holy Spirit), Philip, Prochorus, Nicanor, Timon, Parmenas, Nicolaus of Antioch (a Gentile convert to the Jewish faith, who had become a Christian). These seven were presented to the apostles, who prayed for them and laid their hands on them in blessing.

God's message was preached in ever-widening circles, and the number of disciples increased vastly in Jerusalem; and many of the Jewish priests were converted too.

Stephen, the man so full of faith and the Holy Spirit's power, did spectacular miracles among the people.

But one day some of the men from the Jewish cult of "The Freedmen" started an argument with him, and they were soon joined by Jews from Cyrene, Alexandria in Egypt, and the Turkish provinces of Cilicia, and Ausia. But none of them was able to stand against Stephen's wisdom and spirit.

So they brought in some men to lie about him, claiming they had heard Stephen curse Moses, and even God.

This accusation roused the crowds to fury against Stephen, and the Jewish leaders arrested him and brought him before the Council. The lying witnesses testified again that Stephen was constantly speaking against the Temple and against the laws of Moses.

They declared, "We have heard him say that this fellow Jesus of Nazareth will destroy the Temple, and throw out all of Moses' laws." At this point everyone in the Council chamber saw Stephen's face become as radiant as an angel's!

7

Then the High Priest asked him, "Are these accusations true?"
This was Stephen's lengthy reply: "The glorious God appeared to our ancestor Abraham in Iraq before he moved to Syria, and told him to leave his native land, to say good-bye to his relatives and to start out for a country that God would direct him to. So he left the land of the Chaldeans and lived in Haran, in Syria, until his father died. Then God brought him here to the land of Israel, but gave him no property of his own, not one little tract of land.

"However, God promised that eventually the whole country would belong to him and his descendants—though as yet he had no children! But God also told him that these descendants of his would leave the land and live in a foreign country and there become slaves for 400 years. 'But I will punish the nation that enslaves them,' God told him, 'and afterwards my people will return to this land of Israel and worship me here.'

"God also gave Abraham the ceremony of circumcision at that time, as evidence of the covenant between God and the people of Abraham. And so Isaac, Abraham's son, was circumcised when he was eight days old. Isaac became the father of Jacob, and Jacob was the father of the twelve patriarchs of the Jewish nation. These men were very jealous of Joseph and sold him to be a slave in Egypt. But God was with him, and delivered him out of all of his anguish, and gave him favor before Pharaoh, king of Egypt. God also gave

Joseph unusual wisdom, so that Pharaoh appointed him governor over all Egypt, as well as putting him in charge of all the affairs of the palace.

"But a famine developed in Egypt and Canaan and there was great misery for our ancestors. When their food was gone, Jacob heard that there was still grain in Egypt, so he sent his sons to buy some. The second time they went, Joseph revealed his identity to his brothers, and they were introduced to Pharaoh. Then Joseph sent for his father Jacob and all his brothers' families to come to Egypt, seventy-five persons in all. So Jacob came to Egypt, where he died, and all his sons. All of them were taken to Shechem and buried in the tomb Abraham bought from the sons of Hamor, Shechem's father.

"As the time drew near when God would fulfill his promise to Abraham to free his descendants from slavery, the Jewish people greatly multiplied in Egypt; but then a king was crowned who had no respect for Joseph's memory. This king plotted against our race, forcing parents to abandon their children in the fields.

"About that time Moses was born—a child of divine beauty. His parents hid him at home for three months, and when at last they could no longer keep him hidden, and had to abandon him, Pharaoh's daughter found him and adopted him as her own son, and taught him all the wisdom of the Egyptians, and he became a mighty prince and orator.

"One day as he was nearing his fortieth birthday, it came into his mind to visit his brothers, the people of Israel. During this visit he saw an Egyptian mistreating a man of Israel. So Moses killed the Egyptian. Moses supposed his brothers would realize that God had sent him to help them, but they didn't.

"The next day he visited them again and saw two men of Israel fighting. He tried to be a peacemaker. 'Gentlemen,' he said, 'you are brothers and shouldn't be fighting like this! It is wrong!'

"But the man in the wrong told Moses to mind his own business. 'Who made *you* a ruler and judge over us?' he asked. 'Are you going to kill me as you killed that Egyptian yesterday?'

"At this, Moses fled the country, and lived in the land of Midian, where his two sons were born.

"Forty years later, in the desert near Mount Sinai, an Angel appeared to him in a flame of fire in a bush. Moses saw it and wondered what it was, and as he ran to see, the voice of the Lord called out to him, 'I am the God of your ancestors—of Abraham, Isaac and Jacob.' Moses shook with terror and dared not look.

"And the Lord said to him, 'Take off your shoes, for you are standing on holy ground. I have seen the anguish of my people in Egypt and have heard their cries. I have come down to deliver them. Come, I will send you to Egypt.' And so God sent back the same man his people had previously rejected by demanding, 'Who made *you* a ruler and judge over us?' Moses was sent to be their ruler and savior. And by means of many remarkable miracles he led them out of Egypt and through the Red Sea, and back and forth through the wilderness for forty years.

"Moses himself told the people of Israel, 'God will raise up a Prophet much like me from among your brothers.' How true this proved to be, for in the wilderness, Moses was the go-between—the mediator between the people of Israel and the Angel who gave them the Law of God—the Living Word—on Mount Sinai.

"But our fathers rejected Moses and wanted to return to Egypt. They told Aaron, 'Make idols for us, so that we will have gods to lead us back; for we don't know what has become of this Moses, who brought us out of Egypt.' So they made a calf-idol and sacrificed to it, and rejoiced in this thing they had made.

"Then God turned away from them and gave them up, and let them serve the sun, moon and stars as their gods! In the book of Amos' prophecies the Lord God asks, 'Was it to me you were sacrificing during those forty years in the desert, Israel? No, your real interest was in your heathen gods—Sakkuth, and the star god Kaiway, and in all the images you made. So I will send you into captivity far away beyond Babylon.'

"Our ancestors carried along with them a portable Temple, or Tabernacle, through the wilderness. In it they kept the stone tablets with the Ten Commandments written on them. This building was constructed in exact accordance with the plan shown to Moses by the Angel. Years later, when Joshua led the battles against the

Gentile nations, this Tabernacle was taken with them into their new territory, and used until the time of King David.

"God blessed David greatly, and David asked for the privilege of building a permanent Temple for the God of Jacob. But it was Solomon who actually built it. However, God doesn't live in temples made by human hands. 'The heaven is my throne,' says the Lord through his prophets, 'and earth is my footstool. What kind of home could you build?' asks the Lord. 'Would I stay in it? Didn't I make both heaven and earth?'

"You stiff-necked heathen! Must you forever resist the Holy Spirit? But your fathers did, and so do you! Name one prophet your ancestors didn't persecute! They even killed the ones who predicted the coming of the Righteous One—the Messiah whom you betrayed and murdered. Yes, and you deliberately destroyed God's Laws, though you received them from the hands of angels."

The Jewish leaders were stung to fury by Stephen's accusation, and ground their teeth in rage. But Stephen, full of the Holy Spirit, gazed steadily upward into heaven and saw the glory of God and Jesus standing at God's right hand. And he told them, "Look, I see the heavens opened and Jesus the Messiah standing beside God, at his right hand!"

Then they mobbed him, putting their hands over their ears, and drowning out his voice with their shouts, and dragged him out of the city to stone him. The official witnesses—the executioners—took off their coats and laid them at the feet of a young man named Paul.

And as the murderous stones came hurtling at him, Stephen prayed, "Lord Jesus, receive my spirit." And he fell to his knees, shouting, "Lord, don't charge them with this sin!" and with that, he died.

8

Paul was in complete agreement with the killing of Stephen.

And a great wave of persecution of the believers began that day, sweeping over the church in Jerusalem, and everyone except the apostles fled into Judea and Samaria. (But some godly Jews came and with great sorrow buried Stephen.) Paul was like a wild man, going everywhere to devastate the believers, even entering private homes and dragging out men and women alike and jailing them.

But the believers who had fled Jerusalem went everywhere preaching the Good News about Jesus! Philip, for instance, went to the city of Samaria and told the people there about Christ. Crowds listened intently to what he had to say because of the miracles he did. Many evil spirits were cast out, screaming as they left their victims, and many who were paralyzed or lame were healed, so there was much joy in that city!

A man named Simon had formerly been a sorcerer there for many years; he was a very influential, proud man because of the amazing things he could do—in fact, the Samaritan people often spoke of him as the Messiah. But now they believed Philip's message that Jesus was the Messiah, and his words concerning the Kingdom of God; and many men and women were baptized. Then Simon himself believed and was baptized and began following Philip wherever he went, and was amazed by the miracles he did.

When the apostles back in Jerusalem heard that the people of Samaria had accepted God's message, they sent down Peter and John. As soon as they arrived, they began praying for these new Christians to receive the Holy Spirit, for as yet he had not come upon any of them. For they had only been baptized in the name of the Lord Jesus. Then Peter and John laid their hands upon these believers, and they received the Holy Spirit.

When Simon saw this—that the Holy Spirit was given when the apostles placed their hands upon people's heads—he offered money to buy this power.

"Let me have this power too," he exclaimed, "so that when I lay my hands on people, they will receive the Holy Spirit!"

But Peter replied, "Your money perish with you for thinking God's gift can be bought! You can have no part in this, for your heart is not right before God. Turn from this great wickedness and pray. Perhaps God will yet forgive your evil thoughts—for I can see that there is jealousy and sin in your heart."

"Pray for me," Simon exclaimed, "that these terrible things won't happen to me."

After testifying and preaching in Samaria, Peter and John returned to Jerusalem, stopping at several Samaritan villages along the way to preach the Good News to them too.

But as for Philip, an angel of the Lord said to him, "Go over to the road that runs from Jerusalem through the Gaza Desert, arriving around noon." So he did, and who should be coming down the road but the Treasurer of Ethiopia, a eunuch of great authority under Candace the queen. He had gone to Jerusalem to worship at the Temple, and was now returning in his chariot, reading aloud from the book of the prophet Isaiah.

The Holy Spirit said to Philip, "Go over and walk along beside the chariot."

Philip ran over and heard what he was reading and asked, "Do you understand it?"

"Of course not!" the man replied. "How can I when there is no one to instruct me?" And he begged Philip to come up into the chariot and sit with him.

The passage of Scripture he had been reading from was this:

> "He was led as a sheep to the slaughter, and as a lamb is silent before the shearers, so he opened not his mouth; in his humiliation, justice was denied him; and who can express the wickedness of the people of his generation? For his life is taken from the earth."

The eunuch asked Philip, "Was Isaiah talking about himself or someone else?"

So Philip began with this same Scripture and then used many others to tell him about Jesus.

As they rode along, they came to a small body of water, and the eunuch said, "Look! Water! Why can't I be baptized?"

"You can," Philip answered, "if you believe with all your heart."

And the eunuch replied, "I believe that Jesus Christ is the Son of God."

He stopped the chariot, and they went down into the water and Philip baptized him. And when they came up out of the water, the Spirit of the Lord caught away Philip, and the eunuch never saw him again, but went on his way rejoicing. Meanwhile, Philip found himself at Azotus! He preached the Good News there and in every city along the way, as he traveled to Caesarea.

9

But Paul, threatening with every breath and eager to destroy every Christian, went to the High Priest in Jerusalem. He requested a letter addressed to synagogues in Damascus, requiring their cooperation in the persecution of any believers he found there, both men and women, so that he could bring them in chains to Jerusalem.

As he was nearing Damascus on this mission, suddenly a brilliant light from heaven spotted down upon him! He fell to the ground and heard a voice saying to him, "Paul! Paul! Why are you persecuting me?"

"Who is speaking, sir?" Paul asked.

And the voice replied, "I am Jesus, the one you are persecuting! Now get up and go into the city and await my further instructions."

The men with Paul stood speechless with surprise, for they heard the sound of someone's voice but saw no one! As Paul picked himself up off the ground, he found that he was blind. He had to be led into Damascus and was there three days, blind, going without food and water all that time.

Now there was in Damascus a believer named Ananias. The Lord spoke to him in a vision, calling, "Ananias!"

"Yes, Lord!" he replied.

And the Lord said, "Go over to Straight Street and find the house of a man named Judas and ask there for Paul of Tarsus. He is praying to me right now, for I have shown him a vision of a man named Ananias coming in and laying his hands on him so that he can see again!"

"But Lord," exclaimed Ananias, "I have heard about the terrible things this man has done to the believers in Jerusalem! And we hear that he has arrest warrants with him from the chief priests, authorizing him to arrest every believer in Damascus!"

But the Lord said, "Go and do what I say. For Paul is my chosen instrument to take my message to the nations and before kings, as well as to the people of Israel. And I will show him how much he must suffer for me."

So Ananias went over and found Paul and laid his hands on him and said, "Brother Paul, the Lord Jesus, who appeared to you on the road, has sent me so that you may be filled with the Holy Spirit and get your sight back."

Instantly (it was as though scales fell from his eyes) Paul could see, and was immediately baptized. Then he ate and was strengthened.

He stayed with the believers in Damascus for a few days and went at once to the synagogue to tell everyone there the Good News about Jesus—that he is indeed the Son of God!

All who heard him were amazed. "Isn't this the same man who persecuted Jesus' followers so bitterly in Jerusalem?" they asked. "And we understand that he came here to arrest them all and take them in chains to the chief priests."

Paul became more and more fervent in his preaching, and the Damascus Jews couldn't withstand his proofs that Jesus was indeed the Christ.

After a while the Jewish leaders determined to kill him. But Paul was told about their plans, that they were watching the gates of the city day and night prepared to murder him. So during the night some of his converts let him down in a basket through an opening in the city wall!

Upon arrival in Jerusalem he tried to meet with the believers, but they were all afraid of him. They thought he was faking! Then Barnabas brought him to the apostles and told them how Paul had seen the Lord on the way to Damascus, what the Lord had said to him, and all about his powerful preaching in the name of Jesus. Then they accepted him, and after that he was constantly with the believers and preached boldly in the name of the Lord. But then some Greek-speaking Jews with whom he had argued plotted to murder him. However, when the other believers heard about his danger, they took him to Caesarea and then sent him to his home in Tarsus.

Meanwhile, the church had peace throughout Judea, Galilee and Samaria, and grew in strength and numbers. The believers learned how to walk in the fear of the Lord and in the comfort of the Holy Spirit.

Peter traveled from place to place to visit them, and in his travels came to the believers in the town of Lydda. There he met a man named Aeneas, paralyzed and bedridden for eight years.

Peter said to him, "Aeneas! Jesus Christ has healed you! Get up and make your bed." And he was healed instantly. Then the whole population of Lydda and Sharon turned to the Lord when they saw Aeneas walking around.

In the city of Joppa there was a woman named Dorcas ("Gazelle"), a believer who was always doing kind things for others, especially for the poor. About this time she became ill and died. Her friends prepared her for burial and laid her in an upstairs room. But when they learned that Peter was nearby at Lydda, they sent two men to beg him to return with them to Joppa. This he did; as soon as he arrived, they took him upstairs where Dorcas lay. The room was filled with weeping widows who were showing one another the coats and other garments Dorcas had made for them. But Peter asked them all to leave the room; then he knelt and prayed. Turning to the body he said, "Get up, Dorcas," and she opened her eyes! And when she saw Peter, she sat up! He gave her his hand and helped her up and called in the believers and widows, presenting her to them.

The news raced through the town, and many believed in the Lord. And Peter stayed a long time in Joppa, living with Simon, the tanner.

10

In Caesarea there lived a Roman army officer, Cornelius, a captain of an Italian regiment. He was a godly man, deeply reverent, as was his entire household. He gave generously to charity and was a man of prayer. While wide awake one afternoon he had a vision—it was about three o'clock—and in this vision he saw an angel of God coming toward him.

"Cornelius!" the angel said.

Cornelius stared at him in terror. "What do you want, sir?" he asked the angel.

And the angel replied, "Your prayers and charities have not gone unnoticed by God! Now send some men to Joppa to find a man named Simon Peter, who is staying with Simon, the tanner, down by the shore, and ask him to come and visit you."

As soon as the angel was gone, Cornelius called two of his household servants and a godly soldier, one of his personal bodyguard, and told them what had happened and sent them off to Joppa.

The next day, as they were nearing the city, Peter went up on the flat roof of his house to pray. It was noon and he was hungry, but while lunch was being prepared, he fell into a trance. He saw the sky open, and a great canvas sheet, suspended by its four corners, settle to the ground. In the sheet were all sorts of animals, snakes and birds [forbidden to the Jews for food].

Then a voice said to him, "Go kill and eat any of them you wish."

"Never, Lord," Peter declared, "I have never in all my life eaten such creatures, for they are forbidden by our Jewish laws."

The voice spoke again, "Don't contradict God! If he says something is kosher, then it is."

The same vision was repeated three times. Then the sheet was pulled up again to heaven.

Peter was very perplexed. What could the vision mean? What was he supposed to do?

Just then the men sent by Cornelius had found the house and were standing outside at the gate, inquiring whether this was the place where Simon Peter lived!

Meanwhile, as Peter was puzzling over the vision, the Holy Spirit said to him, "Three men have come to see you. Go down and meet them and go with them. All is well, I have sent them."

So Peter went down. "I'm the man you're looking for," he said. "Now what is it you want?"

Then they told him about Cornelius the Roman officer, a good and godly man, well thought of by the Jews, and how an angel had instructed him to send for Peter to come and tell him what God wanted him to do.

So Peter invited them in and lodged them overnight.

The next day he went with them, accompanied by some other believers from Joppa.

They arrived in Caesarea the following day, and Cornelius was waiting for him, and had called together his relatives and close friends to meet Peter. As Peter entered his home, Cornelius fell to the floor before him in worship.

But Peter said, "Stand up! I'm not a god!"

So he got up and they talked together for a while and then went in where the others were assembled.

Peter told them, "You know it is against the Jewish laws for me to come into a Gentile home like this. But God has shown me in a vision that I should never think of anyone as inferior. So I came as soon as I was sent for. Now tell me what you want."

Cornelius replied, "Four days ago I was praying as usual at this time of the afternoon, when suddenly a man was standing before me clothed in a radiant robe! He told me, 'Cornelius, your prayers are heard and your charities have been noticed by God! Now send some men to Joppa and summon Simon Peter, who is staying in the home of Simon, a tanner, down by the shore.' So I sent for you at once, and you have done well to come so soon. Now here we are, waiting before the Lord, anxious to hear what he has told you to tell us!"

Then Peter replied, "I see very clearly that the Jews are not God's only favorites! In every nation he has those who worship him and do good deeds and are acceptable to him. I'm sure you have heard about the Good News for the people of Israel—that there is peace with God through Jesus, the Messiah, who is Lord of all creation. This message has spread all through Judea, beginning with John the Baptist in Galilee. And you no doubt know that Jesus of Nazareth was anointed by God with the Holy Spirit and with power, and he went around doing good and healing all who were possessed by demons, for God was with him.

"And we apostles are witnesses of all he did throughout Israel and in Jerusalem, where he was murdered on a cross. But God brought him back to life again three days later and showed him to certain witnesses God had selected beforehand—not to the general public, but to us who ate and drank with him after he rose from the dead. And he sent us to preach the Good News everywhere and to testify that Jesus is ordained of God to be the Judge of all—living and dead. And all the prophets have written about him, saying that everyone who believes in him will have their sins forgiven through his name."

Even as Peter was saying these things, the Holy Spirit fell upon all those listening! The Jews who came with Peter were amazed that the gift of the Holy Spirit would be given to Gentiles too! But there could be no doubt about it, for they heard them speaking in tongues and praising God.

Peter asked, "Can anyone object to my baptizing them, now that they have received the Holy Spirit just as we did?" So he did, baptizing them in the name of Jesus, the Messiah. Afterwards Cornelius begged him to stay with them for several days.

11

Soon the news reached the apostles and other brothers in Judea that Gentiles also were being converted! But when Peter arrived back in Jerusalem, the Jewish believers argued with him.

"You fellowshiped with Gentiles and even ate with them," they accused.

Then Peter told them the whole story. "One day in Joppa," he said, "while I was praying, I saw a vision—a huge sheet, let down by its four corners from the sky. Inside the sheet were all sorts of animals, reptiles and birds [which we are not to eat]. And I heard a voice say, 'Kill and eat whatever you wish.'

" 'Never, Lord,' I replied. 'For I have never yet eaten anything forbidden by our Jewish laws!'

"But the voice came again, 'Don't say it isn't right when God declares it is!'

"This happened *three times* before the sheet and all it contained disappeared into heaven. Just then three men who had come to take me with them to Caesarea arrived at the house where I was staying! The Holy Spirit told me to go with them and not to worry about their being Gentiles! These six brothers here accompanied me, and we soon arrived at the home of the man who had sent the messengers. He told us how an angel had appeared to him and told him to send messengers to Joppa to find Simon Peter! 'He will tell you how you and all your household can be saved!' the angel had told him.

"Well, I began telling them the Good News, but just as I was getting started with my sermon, the Holy Spirit fell on them, just as he fell on us at the beginning! Then I thought of the Lord's words when he said, 'Yes, John baptized with water, but you shall be baptized with the Holy Spirit.' And since it was *God* who gave these Gentiles the same gift he gave us when we believed on the Lord Jesus Christ, who was I to argue?"

When the others heard this, all their objections were answered and they began praising God! "Yes," they said, "God has given to the Gentiles, too, the privilege of turning to him and receiving eternal life!"

Meanwhile, the believers who fled from Jerusalem during the persecution after Stephen's death traveled as far as Phoenicia, Cyprus, and Antioch, scattering the Good News, but only to Jews. However, some of the believers who went to Antioch from Cyprus and Cyrene also gave their message about the Lord Jesus to some Greeks. And the Lord honored this effort so that large numbers of these Gentiles became believers.

When the church at Jerusalem heard what had happened, they sent Barnabas to Antioch to help the new converts. When he arrived and saw the wonderful things God was doing, he was filled with excitement and joy, and encouraged the believers to stay close to the Lord, whatever the cost. Barnabas was a kindly person, full of the Holy Spirit and strong in faith. As a result large numbers of people were added to the Lord.

Then Barnabas went on to Tarsus to hunt for Paul. When he found him, he brought him back to Antioch; and both of them stayed there for a full year, teaching the many new converts. (It was there at Antioch that the believers were first called "Christians.")

During this time some prophets came down from Jerusalem to Antioch, and one of them, named Agabus, stood up in one of the meetings to predict by the Spirit that a great famine was coming upon the land of Israel. (This was fulfilled during the reign of Claudius.) So the believers decided to send relief to the Christians in Judea, each giving as much as he could. This they did, consigning their gifts to Barnabas and Paul to take to the elders of the church in Jerusalem.

12

About that time King Herod moved against some of the believers, and killed the apostle James (John's brother). When Herod saw how much this pleased the Jewish leaders, he arrested Peter during the Passover celebration and imprisoned him, placing him under the guard of sixteen soldiers. Herod's intention was to deliver Peter to the Jews for execution after the Passover. But earnest prayer was going up to God from the church for his safety all the time he was in prison.

The night before he was to be executed, he was asleep, double-chained between two soldiers with others standing guard before the prison gate, when suddenly there was a light in the cell and an angel of the Lord stood beside Peter! The angel slapped him on the side to awaken him and said, "Quick! Get up!" And the chains fell off his wrists! Then the angel told him, "Get dressed and put on your shoes." And he did. "Now put on your coat and follow me!" the angel ordered.

So Peter left the cell, following the angel. But all the time he thought it was a dream or vision, and didn't believe it was really happening. They passed the first and second cell blocks and came to the iron gate to the street, and this opened to them of its own accord! So they passed through and walked along together for a block, and then the angel left him.

Peter finally realized what had happened! "It's really true!" he said to himself. "The Lord has sent his angel and saved me from Herod and from what the Jews were hoping to do to me!"

After a little thought he went to the home of Mary, mother of John Mark, where many were gathered for a prayer meeting.

He knocked at the door in the gate, and a girl named Rhoda came to open it. When she recognized Peter's voice, she was so overjoyed that she ran back inside to tell everyone that Peter was standing outside in the street. They didn't believe her. "You're out of your mind," they said. When she insisted they decided, "It must be his angel. [They must have killed him.]"

Meanwhile Peter continued knocking. When they finally went out and opened the door, their surprise knew no bounds. He motioned for them to quiet down and told them what had happened and how the Lord had brought him out of jail. "Tell James and the others what happened," he said—and left for safer quarters.

At dawn, the jail was in great commotion. What had happened to Peter? When Herod sent for him and found that he wasn't there, he had the sixteen guards arrested, court-martialed and sentenced to death. Afterwards he left to live in Caesarea for a while.

While he was in Caesarea, a delegation from Tyre and Sidon arrived to see him. He was highly displeased with the people of those two cities, but the delegates made friends with Blastus, the royal secretary, and asked for peace, for their cities were economically dependent upon trade with Herod's country. An appointment with Herod was granted, and when the day arrived he put on his royal robes, sat on his throne and made a speech to them. At its conclusion the people gave him a great ovation, shouting, "It is the voice of a god and not of a man!"

Instantly, an angel of the Lord struck Herod with a sickness so that he was filled with maggots and died—because he accepted the people's worship instead of giving the glory to God.

God's Good News was spreading rapidly and there were many new believers.

Barnabas and Paul now visited Jerusalem and, as soon as they had finished their business, returned to Antioch, taking John Mark with them.

13

Among the prophets and teachers of the church at Antioch were Barnabas and Symeon (also called "The Black Man"), Lucius (from Cyrene), Manaen (the foster-brother of King Herod), and Paul. One day as these men were worshiping and fasting the Holy Spirit said, "Dedicate Barnabas and Paul for a special job I have for them." So after more fasting and prayer, the men laid their hands on them—and sent them on their way.

Directed by the Holy Spirit they went to Seleucia and then sailed for Cyprus. There, in the town of Salamis, they went to the Jewish synagogue and preached. (John Mark went with them as their assistant.)

Afterwards they preached from town to town across the entire island until finally they reached Paphos where they met a Jewish sorcerer, a fake prophet named Bar-Jesus. He had attached himself to the governor, Sergius Paulus, a man of considerable insight and understanding. The governor invited Barnabas and Paul to visit him, for he wanted to hear their message from God. But the sorcerer, Elymas (his name in Greek), interfered and urged the governor to pay no attention to what Paul and Barnabas said, trying to keep him from trusting the Lord.

Then Paul, filled with the Holy Spirit, glared angrily at the sorcerer and said, "You son of the devil, full of every sort of trickery and villainy, enemy of all that is good, will you never end your opposition to the Lord? And now God has laid his hand of punishment upon you, and you will be stricken awhile with blindness."

Instantly mist and darkness fell upon him, and he began wandering around begging for someone to take his hand and lead him. When the governor saw what happened he believed and was astonished at the power of God's message.

Now Paul and those with him left Paphos by ship for Turkey, landing at the port town of Perga. There John deserted them and returned to Jerusalem. But Barnabas and Paul went on to Antioch, a city in the province of Pisidia.

On the Sabbath they went into the synagogue for the services. After the usual readings from the Books of Moses and from the Prophets, those in charge of the service sent them this message: "Brothers, if you have any word of instruction for us come and give it!"

So Paul stood, waved a greeting to them and began. "Men of Israel," he said, "and all others here who reverence God, [let me begin my remarks with a bit of history].

"The God of this nation Israel chose our ancestors and honored them in Egypt by gloriously leading them out of their slavery. And he nursed them through forty years of wandering around in the wilderness. Then he destroyed seven nations in Canaan, and gave Israel their land as an inheritance. Judges ruled for about 450 years, and were followed by Samuel the prophet.

"Then the people begged for a king, and God gave them Saul (son of Kish), a man of the tribe of Benjamin, who reigned for forty years. But God removed him and replaced him with David as king, a man about whom God said, 'David (son of Jesse) is a man after my own heart, for he will obey me.' And it is one of King David's descendants, Jesus, who is God's promised Savior of Israel!

"But before he came, John the Baptist preached the need for everyone in Israel to turn from sin to God. As John was finishing his work he asked, 'Do you think I am the Messiah? No! But he is coming soon—and in comparison with him, I am utterly worthless.'

"Brothers—you sons of Abraham, and also all of you Gentiles here who reverence God—this salvation is for all of us! The Jews in Jerusalem and their leaders fulfilled prophecy by killing Jesus; for they didn't recognize him, or realize that he is the one the prophets had written about, though they heard the prophets' words read every Sabbath. They found no just cause to execute him, but asked Pilate to have him killed anyway. When they had fulfilled all the prophecies concerning his death, he was taken from the cross and placed in a tomb.

"But God brought him back to life again! And he was seen many times during the next few days by the men who had accompanied him to Jerusalem from Galilee—these men have constantly testified to this in public witness.

"And now Barnabas and I are here to bring you this Good News—that God's promise to our ancestors has come true in our own time, in that God brought Jesus back to life again. This is what the second Psalm is talking about when it says concerning Jesus, 'Today I have honored you as my Son.'

"For God had promised to bring him back to life again, no more to die. This is stated in the Scripture that says, 'I will do for you the wonderful thing I promised David.' In another Psalm he explained more fully, saying, 'God will not let his Holy One decay.' This was not a reference to David, for after David had served his generation according to the will of God, he died and was buried, and his body decayed. [No, it was a reference to another]—someone God brought back to life, whose body was not touched at all by the ravages of death.

"Brothers! Listen! In this man Jesus, there is forgiveness for your sins! Everyone who trusts in him is freed from all guilt and declared righteous—something the Jewish law could never do. Oh, be careful! Don't let the prophets' words apply to you. For they said, 'Look and perish, you despisers [of the truth], for I am doing something in your day—something that you won't believe when you hear it announced.' "

As the people left the synagogue that day, they asked Paul to return and speak to them again the next week. And many Jews and godly Gentiles who worshiped at the synagogue followed Paul and

Barnabas down the street as the two men urged them to accept the mercies God was offering. The following week almost the entire city turned out to hear them preach the Word of God.

But when the Jewish leaders saw the crowds, they were jealous, and cursed and argued against whatever Paul said.

Then Paul and Barnabas spoke out boldly and declared, "It was necessary that this Good News from God should be given first to you Jews. But since you have rejected it, and shown yourselves unworthy of eternal life—well, we will offer it to Gentiles. For this is as the Lord commanded when he said, 'I have made you a light to the Gentiles, to lead them from the farthest corners of the earth to my salvation.' "

When the Gentiles heard this, they were very glad and rejoiced in Paul's message; and as many as wanted eternal life, believed. So God's message spread all through that region.

Then the Jewish leaders stirred up both the godly women and the civic leaders of the city and incited a mob against Paul and Barnabas, and ran them out of town. But they shook off the dust of their feet against the town and went on to the city of Iconium. And their converts were filled with joy and with the Holy Spirit.

14

At Iconium, Paul and Barnabas went together to the synagogue and preached with such power that many—both Jews and Gentiles—believed.

But the Jews who spurned God's message stirred up distrust among the Gentiles against Paul and Barnabas, saying all sorts of evil things about them. Nevertheless, they stayed there a long time, preaching boldly, and the Lord proved their message was from him by giving them power to do great miracles. But the people of the city were divided in their opinion about them. Some agreed with the Jewish leaders, and some backed the apostles.

When Paul and Barnabas learned of a plot to incite a mob of Gentiles, Jews, and Jewish leaders to attack and stone them, they fled for their lives, going to the cities of Lycaonia, Lystra, Derbe, and the surrounding area, and preaching the Good News there.

While they were at Lystra, they came upon a man with crippled feet who had been that way from birth, so he had never walked. He was listening as Paul preached, and Paul noticed him and realized he had faith to be healed. So Paul called to him, "Stand up!" and the man leaped to his feet and started walking!

When the listening crowd saw what Paul had done, they shouted (in their local dialect, of course), "These men are gods in human bodies!" They decided that Barnabas was the Greek god Jupiter, and that Paul, because he was the chief speaker, was Mercury! The local priest of the Temple of Jupiter, located on the outskirts of the city, brought them cartloads of flowers and prepared to sacrifice oxen to them at the city gates before the crowds.

But when Barnabas and Paul saw what was happening they ripped at their clothing in dismay and ran out among the people, shouting, "Men! What are you doing? We are merely human beings like yourselves! We have come to bring you the Good News that you are invited to turn from the worship of these foolish things and to pray instead to the living God who made heaven and earth and sea and everything in them. In bygone days he permitted the nations to go their own ways, but he never left himself without a witness; there were always his reminders—the kind things he did such as sending you rain and good crops and giving you food and gladness."

But even so, Paul and Barnabas could scarcely restrain the people from sacrificing to them!

Yet only a few days later, some Jews arrived from Antioch and Iconium and turned the crowds into a murderous mob that stoned Paul and dragged him out of the city, apparently dead. But as the believers stood around him, he got up and went back into the city!

The next day he left with Barnabas for Derbe. After preaching the Good News there and making many disciples, they returned again to Lystra, Iconium and Antioch, where they helped the believers to grow in love for God and each other. They encouraged them to continue in the faith in spite of all the persecution, reminding them that they must enter into the Kingdom of God through many tribulations. Paul and Barnabas also appointed elders in every church and prayed for them with fasting, turning them over to the care of the Lord in whom they trusted.

Then they traveled back through Pisidia to Pamphylia, preached again in Perga, and went on to Attalia.

Finally they returned by ship to Antioch, where their journey had begun, and where they had been committed to God for the work now completed.

Upon arrival they called together the believers and reported on their trip, telling how God had opened the door of faith to the Gentiles too. And they stayed there with the believers at Antioch for a long while.

15

While Paul and Barnabas were at Antioch, some men from Judea arrived and began to teach the believers that unless they adhered to the ancient Jewish custom of circumcision, they could not be saved. Paul and Barnabas argued and discussed this with them at length, and finally the believers sent them to Jerusalem, accompanied by some local men, to talk to the apostles and elders there about this question. After the entire congregation had escorted them out of the city the delegates went on to Jerusalem, stopping along the way in the cities of Phoenicia and Samaria to visit the believers, telling them—much to everyone's joy—that the Gentiles, too, were being converted.

Arriving in Jerusalem, they met with the church leaders—all the apostles and elders were present—and Paul and Barnabas reported on what God had been doing through their ministry. But then some of the men who had been Pharisees before their conversion stood to their feet and declared that all Gentile converts must be circumcised and required to follow all the Jewish customs and ceremonies.

So the apostles and church elders set a further meeting to decide this question.

At the meeting, after long discussion, Peter stood and addressed them as follows: "Brothers, you all know that God chose me from among you long ago to preach the Good News to the Gentiles, so that they also could believe. God, who knows men's hearts, confirmed the fact that he accepts Gentiles by giving them the Holy Spirit, just as he gave him to us. He made no distinction between them and us, for he cleansed their lives through faith, just as he did ours. And now are you going to correct God by burdening the Gentiles with a yoke that neither we nor our fathers were able to bear? Don't you believe that all are saved the same way, by the free gift of the Lord Jesus?"

There was no further discussion, and everyone now listened as Barnabas and Paul told about the miracles God had done through them among the Gentiles.

When they had finished, James took the floor, "Brothers," he said, "listen to me. Peter has told you about the time God first visited the Gentiles to take from them a people to bring honor to his name. And this fact of Gentile conversion agrees with what the prophets predicted. For instance, listen to this passage from the prophet Amos:

> 'Afterwards' [says the Lord], 'I will return and renew the broken contract with David, so that Gentiles, too, will find the Lord—all those marked with my name.'

That is what the Lord says, who reveals his plans made from the beginning.

"And so my judgment is that we should not insist that the Gentiles who turn to God must obey our Jewish laws, except that we should write to them to refrain from eating meat sacrificed to idols, from all fornication, and also from eating unbled meat of strangled animals. For these things have been preached against in Jewish synagogues in every city on every Sabbath for many generations."

Then the apostles and elders and the whole congregation voted to send delegates to Antioch with Paul and Barnabas, to report on this decision. The men chosen were two of the church leaders—Judas (also called Barsabbas) and Silas.

This is the letter they took along with them:

"*From:* The apostles, elders and brothers at Jerusalem.

"*To:* The Gentile brothers in Antioch, Syria and Cilicia. Greetings!

"We understand that some believers from here have upset you and questioned your salvation, but they had no such instructions from us. So it seemed wise to us, having unanimously agreed on our decision, to send to you these two official representatives, along with our beloved Barnabas and Paul. These men—Judas and Silas, who have risked their lives for the sake of our Lord Jesus Christ—will confirm orally what we have decided concerning your question.

"For it seemed good to the Holy Spirit and to us to lay no greater burden of Jewish laws on you than to abstain from eating food offered to idols and from unbled meat of strangled animals, and, of course, from fornication. If you do this, it is enough. Farewell."

The four messengers went at once to Antioch, where they called a general meeting of the Christians and gave them the letter. And there was great joy throughout the church that day as they read it.

Then Judas and Silas, both being gifted speakers, preached long sermons to the believers, strengthening their faith. They stayed several days, and then Judas and Silas returned to Jerusalem taking greetings and appreciation to those who had sent them. Paul and Barnabas stayed on at Antioch to assist several others who were preaching and teaching there.

Several days later Paul suggested to Barnabas that they return again to Turkey, and visit each city where they had preached before, to see how the new converts were getting along. Barnabas agreed, and wanted to take along John Mark. But Paul didn't like that idea at all, since John had deserted them in Pamphylia. Their disagreement over this was so sharp that they separated. Barnabas took Mark with him and sailed for Cyprus, while Paul chose Silas and, with the blessing of the believers, left for Syria and Cilicia, to encourage the churches there.

16

Paul and Silas went first to Derbe and then on to Lystra where they met Timothy, a believer whose mother was a Christian Jewess but his father a Greek. Timothy was well thought of by the brothers in Lystra and Iconium, so Paul asked him to join them on their journey. In deference to the Jews of the area, he circumcised Timothy before they left, for everyone knew that his father was a Greek [and hadn't permitted this before]. Then they went from city to city, making known the decision concerning the Gentiles, as decided by the apostles and elders in Jerusalem. So the church grew daily in faith and numbers.

Next they traveled through Phrygia and Galatia, because the Holy Spirit had told them not to go into the Turkish province of Ausia at that time. Then going along the borders of Mysia they headed north for the province of Bithynia, but again the Spirit of Jesus said no. So instead they went on through Mysia province to the city of Troas.

That night Paul had a vision. In his dream he saw a man over in Macedonia, Greece, pleading with him, "Come over here and help us." Well, that settled it. We would go to Macedonia, for we could only conclude that God was sending us to preach the Good News there.

We went aboard a boat at Troas, and sailed straight across to Samothrace, and the next day on to Neapolis, and finally reached

Philippi, a Roman colony just inside the Macedonian border, and stayed there several days.

On the Sabbath, we went a little way outside the city to a river bank where we understood some people met for prayer; and we taught the Scriptures to some women who came. One of them was Lydia, a saleswoman from Thyatira, a merchant of purple cloth. She was already a worshiper of God and, as she listened to us, the Lord opened her heart and she accepted all that Paul was saying. She was baptized along with all her household and asked us to be her guests. "If you agree that I am faithful to the Lord," she said, "come and stay at my home." And she urged us until we did.

One day as we were going down to the place of prayer beside the river, we met a demon-possessed slave girl who was a fortune-teller, and earned much money for her masters. She followed along behind us shouting, "These men are servants of God and they have come to tell you how to have your sins forgiven."

This went on day after day until Paul, in great distress, turned and spoke to the demon within her. "I command you in the name of Jesus Christ to come out of her," he said. And instantly it left her.

Her masters' hopes of wealth were now shattered; they grabbed Paul and Silas and dragged them before the judges at the market-place.

"These Jews are corrupting our city," they shouted. "They are teaching the people to do things that are against the Roman laws."

A mob was quickly formed against Paul and Silas, and the judges ordered them stripped and beaten with wooden whips. Again and again the rods slashed down across their bared backs; and afterwards they were thrown into prison. The jailer was threatened with death if they escaped, so he took no chances, but put them into the inner dungeon and clamped their feet into the stocks.

Around midnight, as Paul and Silas were praying and singing hymns to the Lord—and the other prisoners were listening—suddenly there was a great earthquake; the prison was shaken to its foundations, all the doors flew open—and the chains of every prisoner fell off! The jailer wakened to see the prison doors wide open, and assuming the prisoners had escaped, he drew his sword to kill himself.

But Paul yelled to him, "Don't do it! We are all here!"

Trembling with fear, the jailer called for lights and ran to the dungeon and fell down before Paul and Silas. He brought them out and begged them, "Sirs, what must I do to be saved?"

They replied, "Believe on the Lord Jesus and you will be saved, and your entire household."

Then they told him and all his household the Good News from the Lord. That same hour he washed their stripes and he and all his family were baptized. Then he brought them up into his house and set a meal before them. How he and his household rejoiced because all were now believers! The next morning the judges sent police officers over to tell the jailer, "Let those men go!" So the jailer told Paul they were free to leave.

But Paul replied, "Oh, no they don't! They have publicly beaten us without trial and jailed us—and we are Roman citizens! So now they want us to leave secretly? Never! Let them come themselves and release us!"

The police officers reported to the judges, who feared for their lives when they heard Paul and Silas were Roman citizens. So they came to the jail and begged them to go, and brought them out and pled with them to leave the city. Paul and Silas then returned to the home of Lydia where they met with the believers and preached to them once more before leaving town.

17

Now they traveled through the cities of Amphipolis and Apollonia and came to Thessalonica, where there was a Jewish synagogue. As was Paul's custom, he went there to preach, and for three Sabbaths in a row he opened the Scriptures to the people, explaining the prophecies about the sufferings of the Messiah and his coming back to life, and proving that Jesus is the Messiah. Some who listened were persuaded and became converts—including a large number of godly Greek men, and also many important women of the city.

But the Jewish leaders were jealous and incited some worthless fellows from the streets to form a mob and start a riot. They attacked the home of Jason, planning to take Paul and Silas to the City Council for punishment.

Not finding them there, they dragged out Jason and some of the other believers, and took them before the Council instead. "Paul and Silas have turned the rest of the world upside down, and now they are here disturbing our city," they shouted, "and Jason has let them into his home. They are all guilty of treason, for they claim another king, Jesus, instead of Caesar."

The people of the city, as well as the judges, were concerned at these reports and let them go only after they had posted bail.

That night the Christians hurried Paul and Silas to Beroea, and, as usual, they went to the synagogue to preach. But the people of Beroea were more open minded than those in Thessalonica, and gladly listened to the message. They searched the Scriptures day by day to check up on Paul and Silas' statements to see if they were really so. As a result, many of them believed, including several prominent Greek women and many men also.

But when the Jews in Thessalonica learned that Paul was preaching in Beroea, they went over and stirred up trouble. The believers acted at once, sending Paul on to the coast, while Silas and Timothy remained behind. Those accompanying Paul went on with him to Athens, and then returned to Beroea with a message for Silas and Timothy to hurry and join him.

While Paul was waiting for them in Athens, he was deeply troubled by all the idols he saw everywhere throughout the city. He went to the synagogue for discussions with the Jews and the devout Gentiles, and spoke daily in the public square to all who happened to be there.

He also had an encounter with some of the Epicurean and Stoic philosophers. Their reaction, when he told them about Jesus and his resurrection, was, "He's a dreamer," or, "He's pushing some foreign religion."

But they invited him to the forum at Mars Hill. "Come and tell us more about this new religion," they said, "for you are saying some rather startling things and we want to hear more." (I should explain that all the Athenians as well as the foreigners in Athens seemed to spend all their time discussing the latest new ideas!)

So Paul, standing before them at the Mars Hill forum, addressed them as follows:

"Men of Athens, I notice that you are very religious, for as I was out walking I saw your many altars, and one of them had this inscription on it—'To the Unknown God.' You have been worshiping him without knowing who he is, and now I wish to tell you about him.

"He made the world and everything in it, and since he is Lord of heaven and earth, he doesn't live in man-made temples; and human hands can't minister to his needs—for he has no needs! He himself gives life and breath to everything, and satisfies every need there is.

He created all the people of the world from one man, Adam, and scattered the nations across the face of the earth. He decided beforehand which should rise and fall, and when. He determined their boundaries.

"His purpose in all of this is that they should seek after God, and perhaps feel their way toward him and find him—though he is not far from any one of us. For in him we live and move and are! As one of your own poets says it, 'We are the sons of God.' If this is true, we shouldn't think of God as an idol made by men from gold or silver or chipped from stone. God tolerated man's past ignorance about these things, but now he commands everyone to put away idols and worship only him. For he has set a day for justly judging the world by the man he has appointed, and has pointed him out by bringing him back to life again."

When they heard Paul speak of the resurrection of a person who had been dead, some laughed, but others said, "We want to hear more about this later." That ended Paul's discussion with them, but a few joined him and became believers. Among them was Dionysius, a member of the City Council, and a woman named Damaris, and others.

18

Then Paul left Athens and went to Corinth. There he became acquainted with a Jew named Aquila, born in Pontus, who had recently arrived from Italy with his wife, Priscilla. They had been expelled from Italy as a result of Claudius Caesar's order to deport all Jews from Rome. Paul lived and worked with them, for they were tentmakers just as he was.

Each Sabbath found Paul at the synagogue, trying to convince the Jews and Greeks alike. And after the arrival of Silas and Timothy from Macedonia, Paul spent his full time preaching and testifying to the Jews that Jesus is the Messiah. But when the Jews opposed him and blasphemed, hurling abuse at Jesus, Paul shook off the dust from his robe and said, "Your blood be upon your own heads—I am innocent—from now on I will preach to the Gentiles."

After that he stayed with Titus Justus, a Gentile who worshiped God and lived next door to the synagogue. However, Crispus, the leader of the synagogue, and all his household believed in the Lord and were baptized—as were many others in Corinth.

One night the Lord spoke to Paul in a vision and told him, "Don't be afraid! Speak out! Don't quit! For I am with you and no one can harm you. Many people here in this city belong to me." So Paul stayed there the next year and a half, teaching the truths of God.

But when Gallio became governor of Achaia, the Jews rose in

concerted action against Paul and brought him before the governor for judgment. They accused Paul of "persuading men to worship God in ways that are contrary to Roman law." But just as Paul started to make his defense, Gallio turned to his accusers and said, "Listen, you Jews, if this were a case involving some crime, I would be obliged to listen to you, but since it is merely a bunch of questions of semantics and personalities and your silly Jewish laws, you take care of it. I'm not interested and I'm not touching it." And he drove them out of the courtroom.

Then the mob grabbed Sosthenes, the new leader of the synagogue, and beat him outside the courtroom. But Gallio couldn't have cared less.

Paul stayed in the city several days after that and then said goodbye to the Christians and sailed for the coast of Syria, taking Priscilla and Aquila with him. At Cenchreae, Paul had his head shaved according to Jewish custom, for he had taken a vow. Arriving at the port of Ephesus, he left us aboard ship while he went over to the synagogue for a discussion with the Jews. They asked him to stay for a few days, but he felt that he had no time to lose.

"I must by all means be at Jerusalem for the holiday," he said. But he promised to return to Ephesus later if God permitted; and so he set sail again.

The next stop was at the port of Caesarea from where he visited the church [at Jerusalem] and then sailed on to Antioch. After spending some time there, he left for Turkey again, going through Galatia and Phrygia visiting all the believers, encouraging them and helping them grow in the Lord.

As it happened, a Jew named Apollos, a wonderful Bible teacher and preacher, had just arrived in Ephesus from Alexandria in Egypt. While he was in Egypt, someone had told him about John the Baptist and what John had said about Jesus, but that is all he knew. He had never heard the rest of the story! So he was preaching boldly and enthusiastically in the synagogue, "The Messiah is coming! Get ready to receive him!" Priscilla and Aquila were there and heard him—and it was a powerful sermon. Afterwards they met with him and explained what had happened to Jesus since the time of John, and all that it meant!

Apollos had been thinking about going to Greece, and the believers encouraged him in this. They wrote to their fellow-believers there, telling them to welcome him. And upon his arrival in Greece, he was greatly used of God to strengthen the church, for he powerfully refuted all the Jewish arguments in public debate, showing by the Scriptures that Jesus is indeed the Messiah.

19

While Apollos was in Corinth, Paul traveled through Turkey and arrived in Ephesus, where he found several disciples. "Did you receive the Holy Spirit when you believed?" he asked them.

"No," they replied, "we don't know what you mean. What is the Holy Spirit?"

"Then what beliefs did you acknowledge at your baptism?" he asked.

And they replied, "What John the Baptist taught."

Then Paul pointed out to them that John's baptism was to demonstrate a desire to turn from sin to God and that those receiving his baptism must then go on to believe in Jesus, the one John said would come later.

As soon as they heard this, they were baptized in the name of the Lord Jesus. Then, when Paul laid his hands upon their heads, the Holy Spirit came on them, and they spoke in tongues and prophesied. The men involved were about twelve in number.

Then Paul went to the synagogue and preached boldly each Sabbath day for three months, telling what he believed and why, and persuading many to believe in Jesus. But some rejected his message and publicly spoke against Christ, so he left, refusing to preach to them again. Pulling out the believers, he began a separate meeting at the lecture hall of Tyrannus and preached there daily.

This went on for the next two years, so that everyone in the Turkish province of Ausia—both Jews and Greeks—heard the Lord's message.

And God gave Paul the power to do unusual miracles, so that even when his handkerchiefs or parts of his clothing were placed upon sick people, they were healed, and any demons within them came out.

A team of itinerant Jews who were traveling from town to town casting out demons planned to experiment by using the name of the Lord Jesus. The incantation they decided on was this: "I adjure you by Jesus, whom Paul preaches, to come out!" Seven sons of Sceva, a Jewish priest, were doing this. But when they tried it on a man possessed by a demon, the demon replied, "I know Jesus and I know Paul, but who are you?" And he leaped on two of them and beat them up, so that they fled out of his house naked and badly injured.

The story of what happened spread quickly all through Ephesus, to Jews and Greeks alike; and a solemn fear descended on the city, and the name of the Lord Jesus was greatly honored. Many of the believers who had been practicing black magic confessed their deeds and brought their incantation books and charms and burned them at a public bonfire. (Someone estimated the value of the books at $10,000.) This indicates how deeply the whole area was stirred by God's message.

Afterwards, Paul felt impelled by the Holy Spirit to go across to Greece before returning to Jerusalem. "And after that," he said, "I must go on to Rome!" He sent his two assistants, Timothy and Erastus, on ahead to Greece while he stayed awhile longer in Turkey.

But about that time, a big blowup developed in Ephesus concerning the Christians. It began with Demetrius, a silversmith who employed many craftsmen to manufacture silver shrines of the Greek goddess Diana. He called a meeting of his men, together with others employed in related trades, and addressed them as follows:

"Gentlemen, this business is our income. As you know so well from what you've seen and heard, this man Paul has persuaded many, many people that handmade gods aren't gods at all. As a result, our sales volume is going down! And this trend is evident not only here in Ephesus, but throughout the entire province! Of course, I am not only talking about the business aspects of this situation and our loss of income, but also of the possibility that the temple of the great goddess Diana will lose its influence, and that Diana—this magnificent goddess worshiped not only throughout this part of Turkey but all around the world—will be forgotten!"

At this their anger boiled and they began shouting, "Great is Diana of the Ephesians!"

A crowd began to gather and soon the city was filled with confusion. Everyone rushed to the amphitheater, dragging along Gaius and Aristarchus, Paul's traveling companions, for trial. Paul wanted to go in, but the disciples wouldn't let him. Some of the Roman officers of the province, friends of Paul, also sent a message to him, begging him not to risk his life by entering.

Inside, the people were all shouting, some one thing and some another—everything was in confusion. In fact, most of them didn't even know why they were there.

Alexander was spotted among the crowd by some of the Jews and dragged forward. He motioned for silence and tried to speak. But when the crowd realized he was a Jew, they started shouting again and kept it up for two hours: "Great is Diana of the Ephesians! Great is Diana of the Ephesians!"

At last the mayor was able to quiet them down enough to speak. "Men of Ephesus," he said, "everyone knows that Ephesus is the center of the religion of the great Diana, whose image fell down to us from heaven. Since this is an indisputable fact, you shouldn't be disturbed no matter what is said, and should do nothing rash. Yet you have brought these men here who have stolen nothing from her temple and have not defamed her. If Demetrius and the craftsmen have a case against them, the courts are currently in session and the judges can take the case at once. Let them go through legal channels. And if there are complaints about other matters, they can be settled at the regular City Council meetings; for we are in danger of being called to account by the Roman government for today's riot, since there is no cause for it. And if Rome demands an explanation, I won't know what to say."

Then he dismissed them, and they dispersed.

20

When it was all over, Paul sent for the disciples, preached a farewell message to them, said good-bye and left for Greece, preaching to the believers along the way, in all the cities he passed through. He was in Greece three months and was preparing to sail for Syria when he discovered a plot by the Jews against his life, so he decided to go north to Macedonia first.

Several men were traveling with him, going as far as Turkey; they were Sopater of Beroea, the son of Pyrrhus; Aristarchus and Secundus, from Thessalonica; Gaius, from Derbe; and Timothy; and Tychicus and Trophimus, who were returning to their homes in Turkey, and had gone on ahead and were waiting for us at Troas. As soon as the Passover ceremonies ended, we boarded ship at Philippi in northern Greece and five days later arrived in Troas, Turkey, where we stayed a week.

On Sunday, we gathered for a communion service, with Paul preaching. And since he was leaving the next day, he talked until midnight! The upstairs room where we met was lighted with many flickering lamps; and as Paul spoke on and on, a young man named Eutychus, sitting on the window sill, went fast asleep and fell three stories to his death below. Paul went down and took him into his arms. "Don't worry," he said, "he's all right!" And he was! What a wave of awesome joy swept through the crowd! They all went back upstairs and ate the Lord's Supper together; then Paul preached another long sermon—so it was dawn when he finally left them!

Paul was going by land to Assos, and we went on ahead by ship. He joined us there and we sailed together to Mitylene; the next day we passed Chios; the next, we touched at Samos; and a day later we arrived at Miletus.

Paul had decided against stopping at Ephesus this time, as he was hurrying to get to Jerusalem, if possible, for the celebration of Pentecost.

But when we landed at Miletus, he sent a message to the elders of the church at Ephesus asking them to come down to the boat to meet him.

When they arrived he told them, "You men know that from the day I set foot in Turkey until now I have done the Lord's work humbly—yes, and with tears—and have faced grave danger from the plots of the Jews against my life. Yet I never shrank from telling you the truth, either publicly or in your homes. I have had one message for Jews and Gentiles alike—the necessity of turning from sin to God through faith in our Lord Jesus Christ.

"And now I am going to Jerusalem, drawn there irresistibly by the Holy Spirit, not knowing what awaits me, except that the Holy Spirit has told me in city after city that jail and suffering lie ahead. But life is worth nothing unless I use it for doing the work assigned me by the Lord Jesus—the work of telling others the Good News about God's mighty kindness and love.

"And now I know that none of you among whom I went about teaching the Kingdom will ever see me again. Let me say plainly that no man's blood can be laid at my door, for I didn't shrink from declaring all God's message to you.

"And now beware! Be sure that you feed and shepherd God's flock—his church, purchased with his blood—for the Holy Spirit is holding you responsible as overseers. I know full well that after I leave you, false teachers, like vicious wolves, will appear among you, not sparing the flock. Some of you yourselves will distort the truth in order to draw a following. Watch out! Remember the three years I was with you—my constant watchcare over you night and day and my many tears for you.

"And now I entrust you to God and his care and to his wonderful words which are able to build your faith and give you all the inheritance of those who are set apart for himself.

"I have never been hungry for money or fine clothing—you know that these hands of mine worked to pay my own way and even to supply the needs of those who were with me. And I was a constant example to you in helping the poor; for I remembered the words of the Lord Jesus, 'It is more blessed to give than to receive.' "

When he had finished speaking, he knelt and prayed with them, and they wept aloud as they embraced him in farewell, sorrowing most of all because he said that he would never see them again. Then they accompanied him down to the ship.

21

After parting from the Ephesian elders, we sailed straight to Cos. The next day we reached Rhodes and then went to Patara. There we boarded a ship sailing for the Syrian province of Phoenicia. We sighted the island of Cyprus, passed it on our left and landed at the harbor of Tyre, in Syria, where the ship unloaded. We went ashore, found the local believers and stayed with them a week. These disciples warned Paul—the Holy Spirit prophesying through them—not to go to Jerusalem. At the end of the week when we returned to the ship, the entire congregation including wives and children walked down to the beach with us where we prayed and said our farewells. Then we went aboard and they returned home.

The next stop after leaving Tyre was Ptolemais where we greeted the believers, but stayed only one day. Then we went on to Caesarea and stayed at the home of Philip the Evangelist, one of the first seven deacons. He had four unmarried daughters who had the gift of prophecy.

During our stay of several days, a man named Agabus, who also had the gift of prophecy, arrived from Judea and visited us. He took Paul's belt, bound his own feet and hands with it and said, "The Holy Spirit declares, 'So shall the owner of this belt be bound by the Jews in Jerusalem and turned over to the Romans.' " Hearing this, all of us—the local believers and his traveling companions—begged Paul not to go on to Jerusalem.

But he said, "Why all this weeping? You are breaking my heart! For I am ready not only to be jailed at Jerusalem, but also to die for the sake of the Lord Jesus." When it was clear that he wouldn't be dissuaded, we gave up and said, "The will of the Lord be done."

So shortly afterwards, we packed our things and left for Jerusalem. Some disciples from Caesarea accompanied us, and on arrival we were guests at the home of Mnason, originally from Cyprus, one of the early believers; and all the believers at Jerusalem welcomed us cordially.

The second day Paul took us with him to meet with James and the elders of the Jerusalem church. After greetings were exchanged, Paul recounted the many things God had accomplished among the Gentiles through his work.

They praised God but then said, "You know, dear brother, how many thousands of Jews have also believed, and they are all very insistent that Jewish believers must continue to follow the Jewish traditions and customs. Our Jewish Christians here at Jerusalem have been told that you are against the laws of Moses, against our Jewish customs, and that you forbid the circumcision of their children. Now what can be done? For they will certainly hear that you have come.

"We suggest this: We have four men here who are preparing to shave their heads and take some vows. Go with them to the Temple and have your head shaved too—and pay for theirs to be shaved.

"Then everyone will know that you approve of this custom for the Hebrew Christians and that you yourself obey the Jewish laws and are in line with our thinking in these matters.

"As for the Gentile Christians, we aren't asking them to follow these Jewish customs at all—except for the ones we wrote to them about: not to eat food offered to idols, not to eat unbled meat from strangled animals, and not to commit fornication."

So Paul agreed to their request and the next day went with the men to the Temple for the ceremony, thus publicizing his vow to offer a sacrifice seven days later with the others.

The seven days were almost ended when some Jews from Turkey saw him in the Temple and roused a mob against him. They grabbed him, yelling, "Men of Israel! Help! Help! This is the man who preaches against our people and tells everybody to disobey the Jewish laws. He even talks against the Temple and defiles it by bringing Gentiles in!" (For down in the city earlier that day, they had seen him with Trophimus, a Gentile from Ephesus in Turkey, and assumed that Paul had taken him into the Temple.)

The whole population of the city was electrified by these accusations and a great riot followed. Paul was dragged out of the Temple, and immediately the gates were closed behind him. As they were killing him, word reached the commander of the Roman garrison that all Jerusalem was in an uproar. He quickly ordered out his soldiers and officers and ran down among the crowd. When the mob saw the troops coming, they quit beating Paul. The commander arrested him and ordered him bound with double chains. Then he asked the crowd who he was and what he had done. Some shouted one thing and some another. When he couldn't find out anything in all the uproar and confusion, he ordered Paul to be taken to the armory. As they reached the stairs, the mob grew so violent that the soldiers lifted Paul to their shoulders to protect him, and the crowd surged behind shouting, "Away with him, away with him!"

As Paul was about to be taken inside, he said to the commander, "May I have a word with you?"

"Do you know Greek?" the commander asked, surprised. "Aren't you that Egyptian who led a rebellion a few years ago and took 4,000 members of the Assassins with him into the desert?"

"No," Paul replied, "I am a Jew from Tarsus in Cilicia which is no small town. I request permission to talk to these people."

The commander agreed, so Paul stood on the stairs and motioned to the people to be quiet; soon a deep silence enveloped the crowd, and he addressed them in Hebrew as follows:

22

Brothers and fathers, listen to me as I offer my defense." (When they heard him speaking in Hebrew, the silence was even greater.) "I am a Jew," he said, "born in Tarsus, a city in Cilicia, but educated here in Jerusalem under Gamaliel, at whose feet I learned to follow our Jewish laws and customs very carefully. I became very anxious to honor God in everything I did, just as you have tried to do today. And I persecuted the Christians, hounding them to death, binding and delivering both men and women to prison. The High Priest or any member of the Council can testify that this is so. For I asked them for letters to the Jewish leaders in Damascus, with instructions to let me bring any Christians I found to Jerusalem in chains to be punished.

"As I was on the road, nearing Damascus, suddenly about noon a very bright light from heaven shone around me. And I fell to the ground and heard a voice saying to me, 'Saul, Saul, why are you persecuting me?'

" 'Who is it speaking to me, sir?' I asked. And he replied, 'I am Jesus of Nazareth, the one you are persecuting.' The men with me saw the light but didn't understand what was said.

"And I said, 'What shall I do, Lord?'

"And the Lord told me, 'Get up and go into Damascus, and there you will be told what awaits you in the years ahead.'

"I was blinded by the intense light, and had to be led into

Damascus by my companions. There a man named Ananias, as godly a man as you could find for obeying the law, and well thought of by all the Jews of Damascus, came to me, and standing beside me said, 'Brother Saul, receive your sight!' And that very hour I could see him!

"Then he told me, 'The God of our fathers has chosen you to know his will and to see the Messiah and hear him speak. You are to take his message everywhere, telling what you have seen and heard. And now, why delay? Go and be baptized, and be cleansed from your sins, calling on the name of the Lord.'

"One day after my return to Jerusalem, while I was praying in the Temple, I fell into a trance and saw a vision of God saying to me, 'Hurry! Leave Jerusalem, for the people here won't believe you when you give them my message.'

" 'But Lord,' I argued, 'they certainly know that I imprisoned and beat those in every synagogue who believed on you. And when your witness Stephen was killed, I was standing there agreeing—keeping the coats they laid aside as they stoned him.'

"But God said to me, 'Leave Jerusalem, for I will send you far away to the *Gentiles!*' "

The crowd listened until Paul came to that word, then with one voice they shouted, "Away with such a fellow! Kill him! He isn't fit to live!" They yelled and threw their coats in the air and tossed up handfuls of dust.

So the commander brought him inside and ordered him lashed with whips to make him confess his crime. He wanted to find out why the crowd had become so furious!

As they tied Paul down to lash him, Paul said to an officer standing there, "Is it legal for you to whip a Roman citizen who hasn't even been tried?"

The officer went to the commander and asked, "What are you doing? This man is a Roman citizen!"

So the commander went over and asked Paul, "Tell me, are you a Roman citizen?"

"Yes, I certainly am."

"I am too," the commander muttered, "and it cost me plenty!"

"But I am a citizen by birth!"

The soldiers standing ready to lash him, quickly disappeared when they heard Paul was a Roman citizen, and the commander was frightened because he had ordered him bound and whipped.

The next day the commander freed him from his chains and ordered the chief priests into session with the Jewish Council. He had Paul brought in before them to try to find out what the trouble was all about.

23

Gazing intently at the Council, Paul began:

"Brothers, I have always lived before God in all good conscience!"

Instantly Ananias the High Priest commanded those close to Paul to slap him on the mouth.

Paul said to him, "God shall slap you, you whitewashed pigpen. What kind of judge are you to break the law yourself by ordering me struck like that?"

Those standing near Paul said to him, "Is that the way to talk to God's High Priest?"

"I didn't realize he was the High Priest, brothers," Paul replied, "for the Scriptures say, 'Never speak evil of any of your rulers.' "

Then Paul thought of something! Part of the Council were Sadducees, and part were Pharisees! So he shouted, "Brothers, I am a Pharisee, as were all my ancestors! And I am being tried here today because I believe in the resurrection of the dead!"

This divided the Council right down the middle—the Pharisees against the Sadducees—for the Sadducees say there is no resurrection or angels or even eternal spirit within us, but the Pharisees believe in all of these.

So a great clamor arose. Some of the Jewish leaders jumped up to argue that Paul was all right. "We see nothing wrong with him," they shouted. "Perhaps a spirit or angel spoke to him [there on the Damascus road]."

The shouting grew louder and louder, and the men were tugging at Paul from both sides, pulling him this way and that. Finally the commander, fearing they would tear him apart, ordered his soldiers to take him away from them by force and bring him back to the armory.

That night the Lord stood beside Paul and said, "Don't worry, Paul; just as you have told the people about me here in Jerusalem, so you must also in Rome."

The next morning some forty or more of the Jews got together and bound themselves by a curse neither to eat nor drink until they had killed Paul! Then they went to the chief priests and elders and told them what they had done. "Ask the commander to bring Paul back to the Council again," they requested. "Pretend you want to ask a few more questions. We will kill him on the way."

But Paul's nephew got wind of their plan and came to the armory and told Paul.

Paul called one of the officers and said, "Take this boy to the commander. He has something important to tell him."

So the officer did, explaining, "Paul, the prisoner, called me over and asked me to bring this young man to you to tell you something."

The commander took the boy by the hand, and leading him aside asked, "What is it you want to tell me, lad?"

"Tomorrow," he told him, "the Jews are going to ask you to bring Paul before the Council again, pretending they want to get some more information. But don't do it! There are more than forty men hiding along the road ready to jump him and kill him. They have bound themselves under a curse to neither eat nor drink till he is dead. They are out there now, expecting you to agree to their request."

"Don't let a soul know you told me this," the commander warned the boy as he left. Then the commander called two of his officers and ordered, "Get 200 soldiers ready to leave for Caesarea at nine o'clock tonight! Take 200 spearmen and 70 mounted cavalry. Give Paul a horse to ride and get him safely to Governor Felix."

Then he wrote this letter to the governor:

"*From:* Claudius Lysias

"*To:* His Excellency, Governor Felix.

"Greetings! This man was seized by the Jews and they were killing him when I sent the soldiers to rescue him, for I learned that he was a Roman citizen. Then I took him to their Council to try to find out what he had done. I soon discovered it was something about their Jewish beliefs, certainly nothing worthy of imprisonment or death. But when I was informed of a plot to kill him, I decided to send him on to you and will tell his accusers to bring their charges before you."

So that night, as ordered, the soldiers took Paul to Antipatris. They returned to the armory the next morning, leaving him with the cavalry to take him on to Caesarea.

When they arrived in Caesarea, they presented Paul and the letter to the governor. He read it and then asked Paul where he was from.

"Cilicia," Paul answered.

"I will hear your case fully when your accusers arrive," the governor told him, and ordered him kept in the prison at King Herod's palace.

24

Five days later Ananias the High Priest arrived with some of the Jewish leaders and the lawyer Tertullus, to make their accusations against Paul. When Tertullus was called forward, he laid charges against Paul in the following address to the governor:

"Your Excellency, you have given quietness and peace to us Jews and have greatly reduced the discrimination against us. And for this we are very, very grateful to you. But lest I bore you, kindly give me your attention for only a moment as I briefly outline our case against this man. For we have found him to be a troublemaker, a man who is constantly inciting the Jews throughout the entire world to riots and rebellions against the Roman government. He is a ringleader of the sect known as the Nazarenes. Moreover, he was trying to defile the Temple when we arrested him.

"We would have given him what he justly deserves, but Lysias, the commander of the garrison, came and took him violently away from us, demanding that he be tried by Roman law. You can find out the truth of our accusations by examining him yourself."

Then all the other Jews chimed in, declaring that everything Tertullus said was true.

Now it was Paul's turn. The governor motioned for him to rise and speak.

Paul began: "I know, sir, that you have been a judge of Jewish affairs for many years, and this gives me confidence as I make my defense. You can quickly discover that it was no more than twelve days ago that I arrived in Jerusalem to worship at the Temple, and you will discover that I have never incited a riot in any synagogue or on the streets of any city; and these men certainly cannot prove the things they accuse me of doing.

"But one thing I do confess, that I believe in the way of salvation, which they refer to as a sect; I follow that system of serving the God of our ancestors; I firmly believe in the Jewish law and everything written in the books of prophecy; and I believe, just as these men do, that there will be a resurrection of both the righteous and ungodly. Because of this I try with all my strength to always maintain a clear conscience before God and man.

"After several years away, I returned to Jerusalem with money to aid the Jews, and to offer a sacrifice to God. My accusers saw me in the Temple as I was presenting my thank offering. I had shaved my head as their laws required, and there was no crowd around me, and no rioting! But some Jews from Turkey were there (who ought to be here if they have anything against me)—but look! Ask these men right here what wrongdoing their Council found in me, except that I said one thing I shouldn't when I shouted out, 'I am here before the Council to defend myself for believing that the dead will rise again!' "

Felix, who knew Christians didn't go around starting riots, told the Jews to wait for the arrival of Lysias, the garrison commander, and then he would decide the case. He ordered Paul to prison but instructed the guards to treat him gently and not to forbid any of his friends from visiting him or bringing him gifts to make his stay more comfortable.

A few days later Felix came with Drusilla, his legal wife, a Jewess. Sending for Paul, they listened as he told them about faith in Christ Jesus. And as he reasoned with them about righteousness and self-control and the judgment to come, Felix was terrified.

"Go away for now," he replied, "and when I have a more convenient time, I'll call for you again."

He also hoped that Paul would bribe him, so he sent for him from time to time and talked with him. Two years went by in this way; then Felix was succeeded by Porcius Festus. And because Felix wanted to gain favor with the Jews, he left Paul in chains.

25

Three days after Festus arrived in Caesarea to take over his new responsibilities, he left for Jerusalem, where the chief priests and other Jewish leaders got hold of him and gave him their story about Paul. They begged him to bring Paul to Jerusalem at once. (Their plan was to waylay and kill him.) But Festus replied that since Paul was at Caesarea and he himself was returning there soon, those with authority in this affair should return with him for the trial.

Eight or ten days later he returned to Caesarea and the following day opened Paul's trial.

On Paul's arrival in court the Jews from Jerusalem gathered around, hurling many serious accusations which they couldn't prove. Paul denied the charges: "I am not guilty," he said. "I have not opposed the Jewish laws or desecrated the Temple or rebelled against the Roman government."

Then Festus, anxious to please the Jews, asked him, "Are you willing to go to Jerusalem and stand trial before me?"

But Paul replied, "No! I demand my privilege of a hearing before the Emperor himself. You know very well I am not guilty. If I have done something worthy of death, I don't refuse to die! But if I am innocent, neither you nor anyone else has a right to turn me over to these men to kill me. *I appeal to Caesar*."

Festus conferred with his advisors and then replied, "Very well! You have appealed to Caesar, and to Caesar you shall go!"

A few days later King Agrippa arrived with Bernice for a visit with Festus. During their stay of several days Festus discussed Paul's case with the king. "There is a prisoner here," he told him, "whose case was left for me by Felix. When I was in Jerusalem, the chief priests and other Jewish leaders gave me their side of the story and asked me to have him killed. Of course I quickly pointed out to them that Roman law does not convict a man before he is tried. He is given an opportunity to defend himself face to face with his accusers.

"When they came here for the trial, I called the case the very next day and ordered Paul brought in. But the accusations made against him weren't at all what I supposed they would be. It was something about their religion, and about someone called Jesus who died, but Paul insists is alive! I was perplexed as to how to decide a case of this kind and asked him whether he would be willing to stand trial on these charges in Jerusalem. But Paul appealed to Caesar! So I ordered him back to jail until I could arrange to get him to the Emperor."

"I'd like to hear the man myself," Agrippa said.

And Festus replied, "You shall—tomorrow!"

So the next day, after the king and Bernice had arrived at the courtroom with great pomp, accompanied by military officers and prominent men of the city, Festus ordered Paul brought in.

Then Festus addressed the audience: "King Agrippa and all present," he said, "this is the man whose death is demanded both by the local Jews and by those in Jerusalem! But in my opinion he has done nothing worthy of death. However, he appealed his case to Caesar, and I have no alternative but to send him. But what shall I write the Emperor? For there is no real charge against him! So I have brought him before you all, and especially you, King Agrippa, to examine him and then tell me what to write. For it doesn't seem reasonable to send a prisoner to the Emperor without any charges against him!"

26

Then Agrippa said to Paul, "Go ahead. Tell us your story."

So Paul, with many gestures, presented his defense:

"I am fortunate, King Agrippa," he began, "to be able to present my answer before you, for I know you are an expert on Jewish laws and customs. Now please listen patiently!

"As the Jews are well aware, I was given a thorough Jewish training from my earliest childhood in Tarsus and later at Jerusalem, and I lived accordingly. If they would admit it, they know that I have always been the strictest of Pharisees when it comes to obedience to Jewish laws and customs. But the real reason behind their accusations is something else—it is because I am looking forward to the fulfillment of God's promise made to our ancestors. The twelve tribes of Israel strive night and day to attain this same hope I have! Yet, O King, for me it is a crime, they say! But is it a crime to believe in the resurrection of the dead? Does it seem incredible to you that God can bring men back to life again?

"I used to believe that I ought to do many horrible things to the followers of Jesus of Nazareth. I imprisoned many of the saints in Jerusalem, as authorized by the High Priests; and when they were condemned to death, I cast my vote against them. I used torture to try to make Christians everywhere curse Christ. I was so violently opposed to them that I even hounded them in distant cities in foreign lands.

"I was on such a mission to Damascus, armed with the authority and commission of the chief priests, when one day about noon, sir, a light from heaven brighter than the sun shone down on me and my companions. We all fell down, and I heard a voice speaking to me in Hebrew, 'Saul, Saul, why are you persecuting me? You are only hurting yourself.'

" 'Who are you, sir?' I asked.

"And the Lord replied, 'I am Jesus, the one you are persecuting. Now stand up! For I have appeared to you to appoint you as my servant and my witness. You are to tell the world about this experience and about the many other occasions when I shall appear to you. And I will protect you from both your own people and the Gentiles. Yes, I am going to send you to the Gentiles to open their eyes to their true condition so that they may repent and live in the light of God instead of in Satan's darkness, so that they may receive forgiveness for their sins and God's inheritance along with all people everywhere whose sins are cleansed away, who are set apart by faith in me.'

"And so, O King Agrippa, I was not disobedient to that vision from heaven! I preached first to those in Damascus, then in Jerusalem and through Judea, and also to the Gentiles that all must forsake their sins and turn to God—and prove their repentance by doing good deeds. The Jews arrested me in the Temple for preaching this, and tried to kill me, but God protected me so that I am still alive today to tell these facts to everyone, both great and small. I teach nothing except what the prophets and Moses said—that the Messiah would suffer, and be the First to rise from the dead, to bring light to Jews and Gentiles alike."

Suddenly Festus shouted, "Paul, you are insane. Your long studying has broken your mind!"

But Paul replied, "I am not insane, Most Excellent Festus. I speak words of sober truth. And King Agrippa knows about these things. I speak frankly for I am sure these events are all familiar to him, for they were not done in a corner! King Agrippa, do you believe the prophets? But I know you do—"

Agrippa interrupted him. "With trivial proofs like these, you expect me to become a Christian?"

And Paul replied, “Would to God that whether my arguments are trivial or strong, both you and everyone here in this audience might become the same as I am, except for these chains.”

Then the king, the governor, Bernice, and all the others stood and left. As they talked it over afterwards they agreed, “This man hasn’t done anything worthy of death or imprisonment.”

And Agrippa said to Festus, “He could be set free if he hadn’t appealed to Caesar!”

27

Arrangements were finally made to start us on our way to Rome by ship; so Paul and several other prisoners were placed in the custody of an officer named Julius, a member of the imperial guard. We left on a boat which was scheduled to make several stops along the Turkish coast. I should add that Aristarchus, a Greek from Thessalonica, was with us.

The next day when we docked at Sidon, Julius was very kind to Paul and let him go ashore to visit with friends and receive their hospitality. Putting to sea from there, we encountered headwinds that made it difficult to keep the ship on course, so we sailed north of Cyprus between the island and the mainland, and passed along the coast of the provinces of Cilicia and Pamphylia, landing at Myra, in the province of Lycia. There our officer found an Egyptian ship from Alexandria, bound for Italy, and put us aboard.

We had several days of rough sailing, and finally neared Cnidus; but the winds had become too strong, so we ran across to Crete, passing the port of Salome. Beating into the wind with great difficulty and moving slowly along the southern coast, we arrived at Fair Havens, near the city of Lasea. There we stayed for several days. The weather was becoming dangerous for long voyages by then, because it was late in the year, and Paul spoke to the ship's officers about it.

"Sirs," he said, "I believe there is trouble ahead if we go on—perhaps shipwreck, loss of cargo, injuries, and death." But the officers in charge of the prisoners listened more to the ship's captain and the owner than to Paul. And since Fair Havens was an exposed harbor—a poor place to spend the winter—most of the crew advised trying to go further up the coast to Phoenix, in order to winter there; Phoenix was a good harbor with only a northwest and southwest exposure.

Just then a light wind began blowing from the south, and it looked like a perfect day for the trip; so they pulled up anchor and sailed along close to shore.

But shortly afterwards, the weather changed abruptly and a heavy wind of typhoon strength (a "northeaster," they called it) caught the ship and blew it out to sea. They tried at first to face back to shore but couldn't, so they gave up and let the ship run before the gale.

We finally sailed behind a small island named Clauda, where with great difficulty we hoisted aboard the lifeboat that was being towed behind us, and then banded the ship with ropes to strengthen the hull. The sailors were afraid of being driven across to the quicksands of the African coast, so they lowered the topsails and were thus driven before the wind.

The next day as the seas grew higher, the crew began throwing the cargo overboard. The following day they threw out the tackle and anything else they could lay their hands on. The terrible storm raged unabated many days, until at last all hope was gone.

No one had eaten for a long time, but finally Paul called the crew together and said, "Men, you should have listened to me in the first place and not left Fair Havens—you would have avoided all this injury and loss! But cheer up! Not one of us will lose our lives, even though the ship will go down.

"For last night an angel of the God to whom I belong and whom I serve stood beside me, and said, 'Don't be afraid, Paul—for you will surely stand trial before Caesar! What's more, God has granted your request and will save the lives of all those sailing with you.' So take courage! For I believe God! It will be just as he said! But we will be shipwrecked on an island."

About midnight on the fourteenth night of the storm, as we were being driven to and fro on the Adriatic Sea, the sailors suspected land was near. They sounded, and found 120 feet of water below them. A little later they sounded again, and found only ninety feet. At this rate they knew they would soon be driven ashore; and fearing rocks along the coast, they threw out four anchors from the stern and prayed for daylight.

Some of the sailors planned to abandon the ship, and lowered the emergency boat as though they were going to put out anchors from the prow. But Paul said to the soldiers and commanding officer, "You will all die unless everyone stays aboard." So the soldiers cut the ropes and let the boat fall off.

As the darkness gave way to the early morning light, Paul begged everyone to eat. "You haven't touched food for two weeks," he said. "Please eat something now for your own good! For not a hair of your heads shall perish!"

Then he took some hardtack and gave thanks to God before them all, and broke off a piece and ate it. Suddenly everyone felt better and began eating, all two hundred seventy-six of us—for that is the number we had aboard. After eating, the crew lightened the ship further by throwing all the wheat overboard.

When it was day, they didn't recognize the coastline, but noticed a bay with a beach and wondered whether they could get between the rocks and be driven up onto the beach. They finally decided to try. Cutting off the anchors and leaving them in the sea, they lowered the rudders, raised the foresail and headed ashore. But the ship hit a sandbar and ran aground. The bow of the ship stuck fast, while the stern was exposed to the violence of the waves and began to break apart.

The soldiers advised their commanding officer to let them kill the prisoners lest any of them swim ashore and escape. But Julius wanted to spare Paul, so he told them no. Then he ordered all who could swim to jump overboard and make for land, and the rest to try for it on planks and debris from the broken ship. So everyone escaped safely ashore!

28

We soon learned that we were on the island of Malta. The people of the island were very kind to us, building a bonfire on the beach to welcome and warm us in the rain and cold.

As Paul gathered an armful of sticks to lay on the fire, a poisonous snake, driven out by the heat, fastened itself onto his hand! The people of the island saw it hanging there and said to each other, "A murderer, no doubt! Though he escaped the sea, justice will not permit him to live!"

But Paul shook off the snake into the fire and was unharmed. The people waited for him to begin swelling or suddenly fall dead; but when they had waited a long time and no harm came to him, they changed their minds and decided he was a god.

Near the shore where we landed was an estate belonging to Publius, the governor of the island. He welcomed us courteously and fed us for three days. As it happened, Publius' father was ill with fever and dysentery. Paul went in and prayed for him, and laying his hands on him, healed him! Then all the other sick people in the island came and were cured. As a result we were showered with gifts, and when the time came to sail, people put on board all sorts of things we would need for the trip.

It was three months after the shipwreck before we set sail again, and this time it was in *The Twin Brothers* of Alexandria, a ship that had wintered at the island. Our first stop was Syracuse, where we stayed three days. From there we circled around to Rhegium; a day later a south wind began blowing, so the following day we arrived at Puteoli, where we found some believers! They begged us to stay with them seven days. Then we went on to Rome.

The brothers in Rome had heard we were coming and came to meet us at the Forum on the Appian Way. Others joined us at The Three Taverns. When Paul saw them, he thanked God and took courage.

When we arrived in Rome, Paul was permitted to live wherever he wanted to, though guarded by a soldier.

Three days after his arrival, he called together the local Jewish leaders and spoke to them as follows:

"Brothers, I was arrested by the Jews in Jerusalem and handed over to the Roman government for prosecution, even though I had harmed no one nor violated the customs of our ancestors. The Romans gave me a trial and wanted to release me, for they found no cause for the death sentence demanded by the Jewish leaders. But when the Jews protested the decision, I felt it necessary, with no malice against them, to appeal to Caesar. I asked you to come here today so we could get acquainted and I could tell you that it is because I believe the Messiah has come that I am bound with this chain."

They replied, "We have heard nothing against you! We have had no letters from Judea or reports from those arriving from Jerusalem. But we want to hear what you believe, for the only thing we know about these Christians is that they are denounced everywhere!"

So a time was set and on that day large numbers came to his house. He told them about the Kingdom of God and taught them about Jesus from the Scriptures—from the five books of Moses and the books of prophecy. He began lecturing in the morning and went on into the evening!

Some believed, and some didn't. But after they had argued back and forth among themselves, they left with this final word from Paul ringing in their ears: "The Holy Spirit was right when he said through Isaiah the prophet,

" 'Say to the Jews, "You will hear and see but not understand, for your hearts are too fat and your ears don't listen and you have closed your eyes against understanding, for you don't want to see and hear and understand and turn to me to heal you." ' So I want you to realize that this salvation from God is available to the Gentiles too, and they will accept it."

Paul lived for the next two years in his rented house and welcomed all who visited him, telling them with all boldness about the Kingdom of God and about the Lord Jesus Christ; and no one tried to stop him.